A Better Future

How We Fix the World

Tyler True

Dedication

To all of those parents who have broken the cycle of poverty by working hard and sacrificing. Now it's time to finish the job and create a better future for all.

To everyone who wants to live in a better world and are searching for solutions.

Acknowledgment

My mother for always being the safety net I needed when I would continually turn my life upside down with a new career.

Everyone who has been working towards building a better future and laying the foundation of knowledge needed to fix our world.

CONTENTS

Dedication 2

Acknowledgment 2

Introduction 5

Chapter 1: Direct Democracy 14

Chapter 2: Communication 41

Chapter 3: Energy and the Environment.......................48

Chapter 4: Food and Resources 70

Chapter 5: Money and Taxes 88

Chapter 6: Education and Jobs....................................118

Chapter 7: Healthcare and the Elderly 136

Chapter 8: Prison Reform and Law Enforcement............152

Chapter 9: Military and Foreign Policy..........................180

Chapter 10: Immigration, Overpopulation, and Social Assistance..........201

Chapter 11: Entertainment and the Future 220

Chapter 12: How We Get There 235

A Personal Message to You..269

About the Author 273

Introduction

What is the purpose of life? Everyone has a different answer. For some, it's to procreate – to raise little angels in their own angelic image. I personally think we can go deeper than that. For others, it's to live a life without sin so that they can spend eternity in heaven. That doesn't sound very fun, as in you can't spell fun without sin...I think that's how the saying goes. And the idea of spending eternity with only this mind and body sounds a little boring to me, so I'll pass on that one. Some will say there is no point, it's all just chaos and chance – a bunch of bumbling idiots, eating and defecating until we die. That's a tad lazy, but if your life is so difficult that you can't spare any thought to what's possible beyond this realm, then you do what you have to do.

My theory on the purpose of life is quite simple – to experience all that you can in each lifetime and try to always improve. Improve on every aspect of life so that each new life becomes easier, yet also harder because you are challenged with more obstacles, which in turn makes it more satisfying. These obstacles help you get to the point where nothing fazes you as a human and you can conquer anything put in front of you, without crumbling under pressure. Then, you no longer have any purpose of being here – you move on, to where? Perhaps every life form exists to experience all the universe has to offer, and then you become one with everything – God, if you care to use that word. I only know one thing: if being human is all the universe has to offer, then I want my money back, because this show has a pretty unsatisfying ending.

To put it simply: the purpose of life is to get better at life.

To experience all that the earth and the human form has to offer requires freedom; freedom of action, freedom of thought, and freedom of speech. I don't think anyone who has experienced pure freedom could argue that it's possible to live a full life without it. People in China and Russia, for example, have freedom of movement (they can travel to other countries and experience life), they have freedom of thought (as all humans do), but they don't have freedom of speech – to be more specific, freedom of the press.

A free press is what allows citizens in a democratic country to find out the naughty things their leaders do. That knowledge then motivates us to change our leaders when we don't like those corrupt and selfish things they're doing. Ask the people in China or Russia if they have that freedom. Don't go over there to do it, though, because you'll be censored with a noose. Those leaders are there until they get tired of the job or the people revolt. Just because a country has elections does not mean it has democracy, as Russia has shown us.

Democracy and free speech are essential aspects of freedom, something that until recently I thought were untouchable in America. But with the Trump administration, it's become pretty clear that free speech is more fragile than previously thought. This particular president continually attacks journalists when they report the truth. There are proven lies he's said on camera, which he then denies saying, and his supporters don't bat an eyelash. I've personally heard his supporters speak openly that if they had to have a dictator, then Trump would be it. The fact that people will so willingly give up their democracy, their freedom, for the fake promises of prosperity and safety is a troubling thought, to say the least.

The simple truth is that many people across the globe have given up. They've given up having to think or choose. They want to be told what they feel and how to act. The good news is that I think they've gotten this way because they really have had no choice. They've faced a myriad of catastrophes and doomsday news coverage bombarding the average person on a daily basis. What are they supposed to do about it? People get doomsday fatigue and they stop caring – they're only given problems and no solutions.

I mean, vote Democrat or Republican, does it really matter? Does either really offer anything different? It's just a year's campaign worth of worthless platitudes that never amount to anything, once a policy hits the floor of a congressional house paved with wet concrete. What's the point in voting or caring? The one motivating factor getting Americans to vote is our incredible sense of tribalism – North vs. South, East vs. West, and Republican vs. Democrat.

Upon America's inception, it's been us versus us; since the pilgrims arrived trying to bring religion and peace to the natives, and the resource chasers heading west and south for financial prosperity, America has been divided. How can this be solved? It's not easy to tackle the problem of an innate dislike of other citizens in your own country because they have different ideas of what the good life means. Normally, none of this would matter from a global standpoint, except in this case we're talking about the dominant superpower on this planet. The rest of the world watches American politics more than their own, which many Americans don't even realize. It's probably like watching a drunk uncle ruin Christmas by jumping up and down on the table until he face-plants into the turkey.

If nothing changes, then America is headed for another civil war, and it wouldn't just cripple America, it would cripple the world. How do we get drunk Uncle Sam off the sauce that he's been on for 50 years? The sauce being inefficient and wasteful government spending. It's not possible to create policies that are going to make everyone happy, that's not possible in any country. So how do you stop people in Alabama despising people in California and New York for their insane liberal ideals?

You let them govern themselves. I don't mean vote in another career politician who focuses purely on how to win the next election, with zero long-term goals towards sustainability. I mean, the people really govern themselves through direct democracy – online voting. The idea of voting in a representative may have been necessary when you had to travel 100 miles on horseback, and half of your family died on the trek to the voting booth, but it's certainly not necessary now. We, as humans, have the ability to have real democracy for the first time in our evolution, thanks to the internet and ease of communication.

This is obviously no easy task to undertake. First off, you'd have to rip out the entire structure that exists now and plant a whole new seed. A system where the people truly control where their taxes go and what the laws are. That's what democracy is, isn't it? How is it that politicians continually do things that more than 50% of the population doesn't want, and yet there's no easy recourse for us to change it? Should we really have to go into the streets and protest to have them listen to us? Who's actually in charge here? Obviously, the people who have the power are not going to give it up without a fight. The democracies and dictatorships of today have more in common than you might think. They're getting rich off of unsustainable policies that are destroying our health and the health of our planet, all for short-term gain.

There's a psychological study in which they ask young children if they'd like to have one cookie right now, or wait an hour and have 2 cookies. They then studied these children until adulthood. You know what they found? The children who waited for 2 cookies were more successful. That probably doesn't sound all that shocking to you. Yet, if you look at most of your own behaviors, then you'll likely find that you're taking the one cookie in a lot of instances. Any sort of mention of raising your taxes and spittle starts flying out of your mouth with anger. Yet, you want better infrastructure, better healthcare, better education, etc. These things don't come without a cost. But you're not stupid. You know that most of the taxes you pay just get poured down the drain with an inefficient and ambivalent government. I don't blame you for not wanting to put more money into a system like that.

If you asked the average American if they wanted to spend the amount that they do on their military, what do you think most of them would say? I haven't done an actual poll, but I'm pretty sure I know the answer. With healthcare and education costing a fortune, and our infrastructure crumbling, I'm pretty sure they would say, 'let's stop policing the world; it's time to take care of ourselves.' Yet, do the Democrats or Republicans ever offer this option? Trump was all about America first and then he dumped many more billions into the military, while cutting education and environmental protections. That is a weird response to an 'America first' policy.

Why exactly does America need a bigger budget than that of the next 7 biggest militaries combined? It almost seems as if certain powerful individuals are profiting from this. Are Americans worried that China or Russia is going to invade them? That the big and scary superpower of North Korea is going to nuke them? Do Americans really feel that alone in this world? That if a free and democratic nation, any democratic nation on earth, was attacked by a hostile autocracy like Russia, China, Iran, etc., then the other free nations of the world wouldn't join together to fight? Relax, America, take a breather. The future of war on this planet is not bombs and bullets, it's economic warfare – and China is soon to be the new superpower.

If the idea of China ruling the world with an iron fist frightens you, then you're not alone. Why would the budget of their military matter if they control the economy? Once the world is dependent on them, which we essentially already are, they will be the ones to put sanctions on countries and cripple their economies. They'll control us and be able to do whatever they please, with zero recourse for the rest of the world. Are we going to invade China when we don't like what they're doing? Nuke them and have them nuke us, and let's all just nuke the world? That's not going to happen. The overlords want money and power – they don't want the world to end. You no longer get money and power by invading a country or nuking them. This is not the days of the Roman Empire when you could steal a country's resources, and even then it didn't work for long. Military might is not how we win the wars of the future.

Cutting back on military spending is just one option that Americans are never given. There are countless other things that Americans could be spending their taxes on to better their lives and the future of life on this planet...instead of fattening the wallets of politicians and their puppeteers.

I'm not going to throw out a ton of statistics and boring facts for you (just a few). If you're looking for an academic piece with convoluted arguments and big fancy words, then you're going to be greatly disappointed. What I'm going to do is discuss obvious problems, give solutions to those problems, and lay it out for you in simple terms; because I personally like when people speak to me like I'm an idiot. If you want people to see your point, then make it easy for them to understand your argument – I don't need all of your fancy words.

I'm not a political scholar or lifetime academic – I'm a problem solver, an adventurer, a wanderer, and a knowledge seeker. I never stay in anything for long – once the learning curve plateaus, I'm onto the next subject. I think that actually gives me the exact credentials to write such a multi-faceted book as this. But this isn't about my life, I already wrote a book called, 100 WOMEN: A LIFE STORY OF SEX AND

REDEMPTION. That book isn't for mass consumption, like this book is, so stay away from that filth.

Am I qualified to give ideas on how to fix the world? Really, anyone is qualified. It doesn't mean that they're good ideas, or that others are going to listen. I hope you listen to me because I truly believe I have solutions to problems that will help us take the next step in our evolution, ensure our freedom, and create a sustainable and happy population. This book is very straight forward; there won't be anything in here that an average person can't fully comprehend. We can simplify everything and create the world we want, we just have to know what world that is. To me, that is a peaceful world where everyone has what they need to survive, not one controlled by greed. We'll never get there with a system that is controlled by money and purely focused on the next election. Therefore, we have to change the system and take power away from those that have it now.

There are probably few individuals out there who will agree with everything I propose, and that's necessary – if everyone thought the same, then our evolution would stagnate. The point of democracy is for the majority to rule because the majority knows better than the few. That's not always the case, of course, but more often than not, if given truthful information and not misled, then the majority of people know the right thing to do. The majority of people on this planet want world peace – just imagine what we could accomplish as a species if we weren't spending so much money and resources on fighting each other. That may seem like an insurmountable goal at this point in time. But every goal starts with a first step. Luckily, we already took the first step when we got rid of monarchies and adopted a primitive form of democracy – we need to keep doing better. Right now, as a species, we are simply living year to year with no goal in mind – we are only trying to survive. We will never thrive without a long-term goal and plan to get there.

You don't have to buy into everything I'm saying. You don't even have to read all of the chapters in this book that don't interest you; all of the ideas discussed aren't really connected in any way, besides having direct democracy as the root of how to solve the problem. The main purpose of this book is to get you thinking about how to fix the problems facing our long-term survival, if you really had the power to fix them. Right now, we have no power; this is not real democracy taking place in America, or most of the world, it's a sham. The rich control society and they always have. But we live in a time in which we can create real democracy. I assure you that we can do it; you simply have to want it and then read on.

This book will examine how direct democracy could work in a digital age, what needs to change to have a sustainable, highly functioning society, and how we can make it happen.

Chapter 1
Direct Democracy

We see democracy as rule by the people through a representative voted in by the majority. They're supposed to enact laws and policies that directly reflect the constituents' beliefs that voted them in. But how is that possible? How can one person or one party possibly have the same ideology that hundreds of millions of people share? This idea that people are either right-wing or left-wing is ludicrous. It's not that black and white. I, like most people, have some left-wing beliefs and some right-wing beliefs.

I believe in small government that leaves people alone until they can no longer support themselves, or they're negatively affecting other lives on this planet. If a person is taking care of themself, paying taxes, and not bothering anyone else, then I believe the government has no business interfering with how he or she lives their life. I also believe that the government should be investing in the future of its people, through education (skills training), preventative health care, and infrastructure. I believe abortion is a woman's right to choose. I believe a large military is a wasteful use of taxes (I was in the military for 5 years). And I believe there should be an incentive in everything people do (capitalism).

Capitalism is a great thing – it's propelled mankind into an incredibly easy life on this planet. But free-market capitalism is simply not a long-term solution. It requires constant growth and unlimited resources, which obviously this planet can't give us. Pure socialism doesn't work either because there needs to be incentive for people to innovate and work hard. It's basically like being in a union, and anyone that's been in a union knows how toxic that system is for both the company and the employee. Sure it gives you security, but just getting through life should not be our goal. We need the motivation to improve and innovate, to evolve, or else life stagnates. What's the point of working harder than the next person if you're going to get paid the same no matter what? Most humans simply aren't wired to constantly work harder with no extra reward in sight. The two systems are yin and yang (feminine and masculine) and they need to be in balance.

Maybe you agree with some things I believe in and maybe you don't. The point is, no party can ever truly create policies that everyone in a large group will agree with. This idea that you belong to a party, and no matter what they choose to do you have to stand by them, is detrimental to a functioning democracy. You know what else is detrimental to a functioning democracy? Letting a bunch of geriatric judges, who were picked with partisanship in mind, and with lifetime appointments, decide on the most important laws in our society (hi, Supreme Court, I'm talking to you). They terrify me and they should terrify you too. The Supreme Court could make abortion a federal crime, simply because 26% of the eligible voting population voted in a bored narcissist that wants to entertain himself before he croaks. That's not a democracy!

My solution to the lack of power that citizens have, as well as the divide and the tribalism in America, is direct democracy. It's a pretty simple concept, yet nobody is talking about it in the mainstream media. The first step is to change that. Imagine never having to go wait in a lineup to vote again. Imagine if a leader passed a law you didn't agree with and you could instantly go into a voting account and change it (provided the majority felt the same way).

Of course, people can't just vote without some sort of accountability. Otherwise, we'd continue to have what we have now – wasteful spending with repercussions that the future generations will have to deal with. This only works with a voting account attached to your tax account. Every vote you make instantly affects how much taxes you pay. I'll get more into that in the chapter on taxes. For now, let's see how this would work.

First, you have to imagine a third party getting the majority of seats in Congress, and changing the laws to make it possible for people to directly decide where their taxes go. Obviously, this is the hardest step of the entire process and I'll get to this later in the book. For the purposes of this chapter, however, let's just assume that this has happened. After this party takes over Congress, everyone must register to vote – either in person or by emailing documents to the voter registration agency, to verify you are who you say you are. You don't have internet access? There are libraries and many different government stations designed to help you register. Never again should you have to do anything with this account except vote with the click of a button, or update your personal information.

The vast majority of people are already registered and pay taxes, so this should be a pretty simple process for 80% of the population. For the other 20% that somehow don't have any government identification and aren't a part of society, what are you doing walking on sidewalks that you didn't help pay for? In a highly functioning society, everyone has to contribute in some way, unless you're completely incapable of doing anything. But in that case, how are you surviving? Are you on social assistance? Then you're already registered. Are you living in a forest and hunting for food? Then I'm sure you don't own that land and you're breaking the law. Are you begging on the street? Then you should still have to register. And in the system that I'm going to suggest, once you're registered, then the government should be helping you deal with whatever mental illness you have. At the same time, it will be doing the most it possibly can to make you a contributing part of society.

If you refuse to be a part of society, then what are you doing sleeping on a sidewalk you didn't help pay to build? It sounds very harsh to say (this would be the far right-wing part of my beliefs talking – the masculine, survival of the fittest part), but there will come a time in the future when there is no place on earth for people to simply do nothing and use resources. If you're an able-bodied and able-minded person, then you simply have to do something to contribute. This could include cleaning up garbage for a few hours a day, sorting recycling, or sweeping sidewalks – there is literally always something someone can do to help create a better society.

The homeless situation is out of control and will only get worse as the present trend of economic inequality continues. Many politicians seem more concerned with staying out of the way of difficult choices and doing just enough to get re-elected. They don't seem concerned with making actual changes. We're going to need to make hard choices when it comes to some individuals who simply want a free ride. It's the same as being in a union, doing as little as possible is neither good for the individual's soul, nor the society that individual lives in. It's toxic for all involved and the bleeding hearts will not be able to save everyone.

Let's be clear, I am one of those bleeding hearts; however, I can turn it off for the sake of pragmatism and the belief that you have to sacrifice the few to save the many. We can't continue to spend incredible resources on individuals who have no desire to participate in a healthy society, that's just not the way nature works. Despite what humans may think, we have to follow the rules of nature, or nature will force its rules on us, and it won't be pretty. Some people are definitely going to fight this step, but every single person in America must register for a government account.

Now, how would votes come up in this system? Here is my thought: no matter who you are, you can put in a suggestion for a vote. Let's jump right into it with something big like the decriminalization of drugs. This suggestion gets sent out to 1000 people. If more than half of them think it's worth voting on, then it goes into the queue. If not, it gets thrown out. There's also the option to vote on it immediately, or let it wait its turn in the order it was received. Let's say someone puts in a suggestion like, 'we should kill all foreigners in our country,' and it gets sent out to 1000 people. If more than half of those people claim that this person should not be allowed to make voting suggestions (and should probably seek therapy), then that person loses their right to send in proposals. This could be for a year or two...or until they get help.

Now, let's go with something smaller: someone wants to build a new school in their district or fix a road that's littered with potholes. These are likely too small of decisions to be voted on, as your representative (or district manager) will have a budget allocated for these sorts of things, and the people shouldn't be bothered with mundane maintenance. Instead, the government should be treated like all other services – they get a rating from the people who use that service. If the roads in a certain district are horrible, then the people will give that service a thumbs down. If the leader in charge of that district doesn't take care of that problem, and has too many low ratings on services offered, then they will likely lose their job.

If you don't want to spend a few minutes a day being a part of this voting process, then you can give your vote away. I foresee many different parties coming into the picture that more accurately coincide with particular people's beliefs. They'll likely charge you for doing your job; perhaps something like $50 a year. If they don't charge you for doing your job, and you don't personally know them, then be wary because they are likely just doing it for selfish purposes. Even if you give your vote to a party, you should still be able to easily go into the system and change a vote, if you don't like what they did.

If you refuse to take part in the process, then you'll get an increase in your taxes as a fine. Some countries, like Australia, fine their citizens for not voting. In the 2-party system that's taken over America, I personally don't see the point in that. But if we create a system that demands participation from the population, then you'd have to incentivize people to do their job. Not all senators and congressmen have to vote on every bill, so citizens shouldn't either – perhaps something like 60% participation or they get fined.

There would be three separate votes: district, state, and federal. Everyone will pay different taxes depending on where they live and what their fellow constituents have voted on.

Say a vote for a new task comes up in your district: let's get the homeless off of the street. The voting service objectively shows the pros and cons of each vote. Pros: reduce crime and drug use, create productive citizens in society, heal mental illness (as best as we can), make people feel safer while walking at night. The list could go on. Con: your taxes will go up by 1% until the problem is under control.

Another vote: decriminalization of drugs. Pros: you will save a great deal in taxes from putting people in prison for drug-related crimes and the cost of the war on drugs. That money can then be used to treat those with addiction problems, with the goal of turning them into productive citizens. This is contrary to throwing your money in the garbage by putting them in prison and turning them into lifelong criminals (that point may not have been worded so objectively). We can make money off of taxes from selling drugs instead of that money going into the black market. You end the power of drug cartels, thereby helping Central and South America to heal themselves. The act of doing drugs becomes less appealing for some if you're not breaking the law. This list of pros could go on for a while. Con: drug use may go up if children aren't educated properly about the dangers. I have a hard time thinking of more cons, to be honest.

I personally think the war on drugs has done more damage to more people, for a longer period of time, than either of the two world wars. Central and South America are disasters mainly because of this war, and they've been this way since the war was escalated 40 years ago. But this is not the chapter for that discussion.

How about who comes up with the estimates for how much each task would cost? Let's say the vote to get all homeless off of the street has come up – more than 50% of the people think it's worthy of voting on. It then goes into a system where contractors can bid on that project. The job of the government would then be to calculate how much it would cost the taxpayers to get this task done.

Let's say a drug rehabilitation clinic projects that it'll cost $20,000 a person to treat, and there is an average of 500 people living on the street in a district – that would cost ten million dollars just for drug rehabilitation. There is also the cost of training them in a certain skill (although, with the system I'm proposing this would already be in the budget), the cost of housing them, feeding them, and continued monitoring and drug testing. Let's say that they determine the total cost to come out to $150,000 per person for 2 years of rehabilitation; which equals 75 million dollars.

The cost is determined and compared to the taxes paid in that district. It's calculated that we would need an increase of 1% of everyone's taxes in that district to pay for this program. That's what the vote would say – to treat everyone on the street and train them to join the workforce would require a 1% (for most individuals that would be about $250 a year) increase in your taxes.

Saying all of that, a problem of this magnitude would be much better placed as a federal vote. I say that because some districts or states could be quite ruthless, which would force all of the homeless to migrate to a more compassionate area – that's a problem. Also, federal taxes would have to be raised by less to fix this issue. And what tax paying citizen doesn't want to fix this issue? Plus, the majority of homeless live in coastal states, but they come from all over America; it should be everyone's responsibility to deal with. However, the federal government should never actually be in charge of a task, they're simply there to distribute money to the smallest entity as efficiently as possible.

The governing body in charge of this would also have to consider the amount of money we already put into homeless people, through healthcare and law enforcement costs. Right now, we pay approximately $30,000 a year per homeless person through various expenditures, without any sort of payback in sight. We're covering up the symptoms instead of tackling the root of the issue – this is what's happening with pretty much every problem in the world.

Of course, not all homeless people will accept this, many probably won't, and that problem will be discussed later. As a little taste, a vote of what to do with those individuals who refuse treatment would look something like this: do you want to pay to institutionalize those that refuse to be a part of society at an indefinite increase of 1% of your taxes, or do you want to euthanize these people? Sounds insane, I realize, but difficult decisions have to be made to create balance and sustainability. We simply can't afford to keep going into debt, not raise taxes to pay for the left-wing programs that people want, and put Band-Aids on problems without actually paying for it at some point.

The majority will always have the choice in what they want to do – pay more taxes to put people away for life, save taxes by euthanizing them, or continue as we are with a much greater cost coming down the road. Many people will choose to wait to act until they're forced to. The two cookie eaters have to outnumber those people, or else society is in for some very hard lessons. Either way, if they decide to do nothing, then they're still going to be paying for it. They'll just be paying indefinitely with no possible chance of return of investment. Going into more debt is no longer an option – that's now against the law because you're negatively impacting the next generations. I should rephrase that, going into more foreign owned debt is now against the law. We will still have publicly owned debt, except now we're going to have a plan to pay it back. We'll get to that.

I believe the majority would vote to raise their taxes to keep people institutionalized instead of euthanizing them – judging from initial reactions I've gotten from people regarding this topic. No matter what, I believe society will at least give these destitute souls a chance to heal themselves. To me, that's the most important step in this task. If they refuse to try, then what right do they have in demanding that society look after them?

Theoretically, contracts on tasks like this should go to the lowest bidder, but that may not always be the best option, especially if it's ridiculously underbid. Either way, this is the job of the DISTRICT MANAGER to decide. A district manager is your elected official; equivalent to your congressperson. A lot of their job will be the same as it is now, except that they're not actually deciding on laws and policies. They won't be sitting in sessions with other congress members to argue over policies and tax allocation that never amounts to anything. They're just there to get done what the people in a district have tasked them to do, and to find the right people to get those jobs done.

Senators would also have a lot of the same responsibilities as now, except we would only need one per state. The only people allowed to run for senator should be lawyers who have worked for the district or state attorney's office with a minimum of 5 years experience. They are the law writers and they would need a team to help them with that – the size of the team would be dependent on the size of their state. They would write the laws that a district, state or federal vote has put into place. They need to make sure whatever laws we want to enact follow the Constitution and the Bill of Rights. They are the ones that will be defending or prosecuting these laws in court. They would also essentially be in charge of the judicial system, watchdogs for corruption, and appointing judges to the high courts. Although, I think it would be better to have the judicial branch develop a voting system where they appoint judges themselves – they know better than anyone who would make the best judges.

The job of a president, governor, or mayor will also be very similar to what it is now, except that they won't technically have any power to create laws or policies...unless the majority has given them their vote. These people would need a lot less protection since they technically wouldn't hold any power, and we could save billions on the Secret Service. These officials would be there to ensure the smooth operation of districts/states, distribute wealth and resources between districts/states, put new money into the system, allocate people to different positions in their respective governments, implement diplomacy between countries, and deal with emergencies. We can also strip the federal government of a lot of useless, top-heavy positions that decrease efficiency and leave states and districts to truly govern themselves...until they've shown that they can't.

All of these positions are still incredibly important. We will create a system where the elections for president, district manager, senator etc, would be staggered, and only called for at the request of the majority; instead of the lower appointees just being brushed off to the side during our current elections. We will create a system where an elected official only has to worry about doing a good job, and not worry about winning the next election. There should only be an election if that individual has proven to be incompetent and the people call for an election. I would hope that these positions will evolve to go to people who are better at planning and executing than at being a politician. We do this by giving them a report card at the end of every year – a pass or fail on everything they were tasked to get done that was completed on time and on budget. If they get a fail on a certain task, then they should be able to explain in a short and easy to read paragraph what happened. If they get a satisfactory report card, then they will probably keep their position. If they fail on too many tasks, or if too many government services have a negative rating, then it's likely the people will call for a new election.

Have you ever dealt with a government employee? Are they concerned about giving good service and being pleasant? I didn't think so. They feel invincible. They've forgotten they work for us. We need to start rating them like every other industry is subject to and if a government service has a low rating, then that will reflect on that elected appointee. This also applies to government websites. Have you ever tried to use a government website? I feel your pain. What incentive do they have to create a user-friendly interface? We can fix that.

A district manager's primary job is to get things done and create better government services, while using as small a budget as possible...something that most of our current elected officials would likely not be very good at. This job should pay well and come with incentives for getting tasks done on time and on budget. This job has to attract the most capable and efficient managers out there – always remember that you get what you pay for.

They should also have a daily ledger of what they've done every single day that's put online for their constituents to see. The government should always make it easily visible, and in plain language, what they're doing. We are their boss. In what job does an employee get to do what they want in a day and report to their boss only when they feel like it? Or make their reports so vague or convoluted that the boss won't bother? That has to end.

What if the employees lie? Well, that's treason, is it not? Any time a government employee talks to the public, it should be the same as being under oath. We want to have the stiffest penalties in place for people in government, unlike now where they get a slap on the wrist for some pretty severe crimes; like starting a 20-year war under false pretenses in order to steal tax payer money. Case in point, Iraq. We want to weed out the people who want this job for power and influence, which is kind of the opposite of what a position in political office attracts now. We want to attract only people who are truthful and wouldn't worry about getting in trouble – those that think they can get in and cheat the public will learn pretty quickly that it's not worth the risk.

Let's get back to these contractors bidding on the tasks. In a system like this, companies would emerge that become trusted to do things well and affordably. If a company makes a bid, and they're unable to complete the job on time and on budget, then they lose their ability to bid on another project for a year or two. If they do a completely negligent job, or are obviously there to just collect the money and run, then they face criminal charges, not unlike treason. Again, this should not be a place to make money where liars and cheaters are attracted to. Stiff penalties for trying to cheat the people would be very necessary.

I honestly believe in a system like this we would create more jobs, get a lot more done fixing our infrastructure, and spend the same amount of money as we do now on our wasteful governments that get very little done. We need to have capitalism dominate infrastructure projects, instead of turning these workers into government employees. Just imagine it, road workers actually fixing the roads, instead of dragging it out for as long as possible.

Let's say a vote happens that didn't go your way, how is it possible for that law or policy to ever change? Example: a law gets passed that bans assault rifles. A person can disagree and click an option that says, 'I want a re-vote.' If enough people click on that option (let's say more people than the number it took to make that law happen), then there's a re-vote. All of those people that wanted a re-vote are then charged $1 in their tax account, for administrative costs. It would be the same process for new elections.

On a state level, I feel that votes would more often be about actual laws than projects to be completed. The smaller an entity is, the more efficient it can be in getting jobs done. The government, as it stands now, wastes an incredible amount of money on red tape and bureaucracy. This is one of the reasons why I think it should come down to the district level to truly govern themselves, as far as infrastructure and fixing problems like homelessness and social assistance are concerned. State and Federal taxes would likely become a fairly stable amount, and district taxes would be where you really decide where your money goes.

Of course, some districts are poorer than others, and that's where the state and federal department comes in – to distribute wealth and resources where they're needed most. It's also quite possible to redraw districts to make them equitable in wealth. At the very least, the first thing that should be done is to redraw districts in a completely arbitrary fashion, as in blocks that are sorted by the number of people and not by their political beliefs. What Republicans have done with redrawing districts to ensure that they have the numbers in the Electoral College is a criminal act, and somehow they aren't paying for it. Democrats do the same thing when they have the power. It's a broken system, and you might hear that a few times in this book.

On the federal level, it would mostly be about the military, and we would have to vote in a military leader. To have a career politician act as the military leader is a bit nonsensical, don't you think? It made sense when they wrote the Constitution, but it's now one of many outdated laws that needs to be changed. Federal votes would also constitute federal laws and foreign policy. However, I would urge the American people to limit the number of federal laws. If you want to prevent a civil war, then you'll let the 'less progressive' states govern themselves. If there was a federal vote on something like abortion, of course the majority would be pro-choice. But what is that majority? 60%? I personally don't think that's enough for a federal law. There would be many religious districts that would be much easier to convince to adopt this system if they were finally able to truly govern themselves.

Let them make their own archaic laws. If you live in a place that makes laws you don't like, then move to another district or state. We can create low interest loans to help people do that. I personally don't see a problem with allowing groups of like-minded individuals to cohabitate in the same region. That seems like real democracy to me. There will be districts and states that do a lot of dumb things, and they'll pay for it. They'll see how more progressive areas have made changes that have improved everyone's lives and attracted the young to move there, instead of continuing to live with outdated ideologies. Those people struggling to survive in these 'dark zones' will come around, or they'll sink even further. If they ask for help from a higher governing body, then they've just lost their right to govern themselves.

It'll be pretty obvious in not too long with regards to what is working and what isn't. If a district or state refuses to adapt, and they're unable to support themselves, then they lose their right to govern themselves – the same as an individual human. They won't be able to create their own money so they'll have to go to the federal government. The great thing about life is, nothing stays bad and nothing stays good. People will hit rock bottom and be forced to make changes. Just like areas that are doing really well will be forced to keep adapting, because nothing stays the same. You adapt or die.

The reason why Europe and Asia evolved so much faster than the Americas or Africa is not because of intelligence or race. It was simply because those civilizations were able to learn from each other. The Silk Road made it possible for people from Britain to travel all the way to Asia, and to learn what those other civilizations were doing better than them. People in Africa and the Americas didn't have that luxury – they were trapped due to physical boundaries like mountain ranges or deserts. This is also how real democracy will evolve. Federal and state votes should not hamper the ability for districts to come up with new and innovative ways to spend their money, or make money. I think we'll see some pretty ingenious ideas if that many people are given unencumbered autonomy to govern themselves and innovate.

It doesn't just stop at districts or states learning from each other – what about other countries that have policies that are obviously benefiting their citizens? It's pretty clear to anyone paying attention that there are Scandinavian countries doing quite well year after year in both their economy and quality of life metrics. Denmark consistently places near the top of every list in terms of quality of life, happiness, and their spending power. America, on the other hand, consistently places 3rd last in happiness ratings, behind only China and India. Is the economy more important than happiness?

Why does America not adopt some of Europe's policies? It's not a secret that countries that invest in their people over their military have a better quality of life, even though their gross domestic product (GDP) is lower (which is a ridiculous metric that we'll explore later). Take Germany, for example, they are a country filled with skilled workers and they produce top of the line products. Why? It's because they invest in their people to learn. I'm not saying everything they do is ideal, such as forcing people down specific paths, but certainly some of their policies could be adopted.

Now, we come to the most difficult aspect regarding convincing people to adopt this system – everything I'm suggesting requires rewriting the Constitution. Americans pledge allegiance to their Constitution every day and nationalism is basically like their religion. In case you didn't know, changing someone's religion, or their fundamental beliefs, is about the most difficult thing in the world to do. Americans have been indoctrinated with the belief that the Constitution is the basis for their freedom, and it's going to be difficult to convince them otherwise. They need to know that the Bill of Rights is an add-on to the original constitution and shouldn't need to be changed – that's where the real protections for citizens are. The original Constitution simply dictates the authority of the government and how it functions, and that's what we want to change. Every time I talk about the Constitution in this book, I'm referring to the Articles written regarding government structure, not the Bill of Rights – which is amazing. The Constitution has ended up creating a corrupt and inefficient system that is opposite to democracy. If you think the founding fathers would be happy with how the current government is functioning, then you are blinded by your religion. They would be appalled that we haven't already fixed this disaster.

We should be pledging allegiance to freedom, to happiness, to a sustainable future, and to constantly evolving democracy – not to a system that is being held hostage by the wealthy. The original Constitution was necessary for that time, but we need to adapt it in order to work in this technological age. The rotten roots need to be ripped out and a new system replanted. Iceland did it after the 2008 crash – America can do it too.

This chapter on direct democracy does not go into detail on taxes, military, or anything else of substance – it's all coming. This chapter is simply about discussing the idea of online voting. If you don't like the idea of having direct control over our legislators, then nothing else in this book matters, because politicians will never willingly make the changes needed to fix our world. If you're worried about voter fraud, don't be. With a voter account attached to an actual tax payer's account, it will be near impossible to create false identities, at least not in the numbers they would need to alter policies. There are other things we can use, like block-chain technology. Or, make your vote visible for everyone to see – pretty hard to falsify that.

If you're worried that the poor, who pay no taxes, can vote to take away everything from those that have worked hard for what they have, then worry not, I will discuss this in short order. There are a million details that would not fit in this book, but trust me when I say that there are solutions to every problem. People are going to make mistakes. They're going to vote impulsively and with emotion, instead of a balance between heart and mind. They're going to sometimes vote through fear instead of logic. They're going to try and spend as little as possible and their infrastructure will crumble. But they're going to learn. They're going to pay for their mistakes and they'll get better at governing themselves.

There is no perfect solution to anything that life throws at us. There is always a balance between good and bad. There is only one constant in the universe and that is change – the sine wave, cyclical pattern of up and down. We don't get to constantly go up, but that also means we don't ever constantly go down. The goal of all life and energy is balance – to stop having the erratic ups and downs.

Right now, our population is on a steep upward trajectory in population, which, not so coincidentally, coincides with a steep downward trajectory in sustainability. If you think that we can sustain what's happening in this world indefinitely, then you and I probably wouldn't agree on much in life. We either ignore the laws of the universe and let it decide when and how hard the crash is going to be, or we learn from history and take our future into our own hands. We can slow the eventual and inevitable downward curve in the population that is coming. Or, we can continue like we are, leaving the power in the hands of those that will take and take until there's nothing left (because it's an addiction for them). This would result in a free-fall into chaos and destruction.

The system I describe demands participation and accountability. Right now, many in America want to blame politicians for everything that's wrong with the country, and in a way they're right to do so – they're doing an incredibly terrible job at pretty much everything they touch. But it's not just their fault. The system was inadvertently designed to attract those types of greedy, power-hungry individuals. More importantly, citizens of democratized countries have not really had any other options until the internet became mainstream. Our tribalism has also kept us blinded to the other possibilities besides democrat or republican. Everyone has a bit of blame to take in this broken system.

Unfortunately, if you make the wrong decision and a vote gets put into action that turns into a disaster, then you'll have no one to blame but yourself. That probably terrifies a lot of people. They like the idea of passing the blame onto someone else. But that's not what evolution has in store for mankind. We're meant to control our own lives and our own destinies; to live our fullest life, not being controlled by politicians, even if it means we screw up from time to time.

The point of this system is not to have everyone spending all of their time voting – there's no question that most people don't want to do that. Some districts will likely vote in a competent and trustworthy individual who has the best interests of their constituents at heart. That doesn't simply mean the immediate interests, but the long-term profitability and sustainability of their district. Many districts will find incredible people that they trust and they give the majority of their votes to. These people will develop trans-formative policies that catapult their districts into the plus – and if every district is in the black (profitable), then America is in the black.

These innovative and progressive individuals will lead the charge towards a more highly functioning government. Other districts will need to change policies that aren't working for them, and they'll see what's working in other districts. If districts have systems in place that are crippling their economies, then they'll need to change those policies in order to get help. The point of this system is not to make your life harder; it's to give people direct and immediate control over policies and laws, if their elected manager does something that they don't like.

There will be a lot of talk about the Constitution and what it means if the people can all of a sudden make whatever laws they want. First of all, in order to change the Constitution in America, you need ⅔ of Congress to sign off on it, which will be difficult to do for some time...I hope I'm wrong. Second of all, we will create a system of government that is adaptive and always makes sure the people have control over what laws they want to enact, but also ensures the rights of every citizen; again, we need to make it very clear that we are not going to change the Bill of Rights, only the power that government has over the people. To do that, we will need to rewrite the Constitution upon getting enough seats in Congress. Here are some plainly written Articles that I think the Direct Democracy Party could run on:

Article I: Residents of America shall decide their laws, policies, and tax allocation directly, without the need for representation, through whatever form of efficient communication is considered widely available at the time. A voting account must be joined with a tax account, while every vote shall directly reflect future taxation. The people shall also be able to give their vote to another party of their choosing. However, the conclusive vote shall never be withheld from that individual.

This first Article essentially goes against everything that the current Constitution is based on. The American Constitution is purely focused on a president, House of Representatives, and Senate controlling legislation, which I think we can all agree is not working. Therefore, until the Constitution can be rewritten, we'll have to use Congress as our middlemen in order to make legislation. I personally can't see any law we could write that would give direct and immediate control to the people without changing the Constitution.

Article II: District managers, state governors, mayors, state

senators, the military general, and the president will be elected by the majority in their respective voting blocs. It will take 2 elections for a representative to be elected. The 2nd election will be based solely on the top 2 representatives from the 1st election. An election will take place upon the request of 51% of the residents in that respective voting bloc. Election campaigns shall not last longer than 2 months after an election is called for, with the 2 elections separated by 1 month. Only citizens and permanent residents of at least 18 years of age shall have the right to vote. Any citizen residing in America of at least 30 years of age may acquire any position in government. A declaration of war will solely be placed on the citizens of America, through a majority vote; unless, America is under physical attack. In which case, the elected military general has the authority to take any necessary actions to defend America against further harm – until a vote for war has been concluded.

This Article gives adaptability for many things, such as how many districts we have. It may be more practical and efficient to have more districts and less senators. It also gives adaptability in terms of what each of these appointments is in charge of. We have to create a system that allows quick and easy adaptation.

Article III: It will take 70% of a national vote to add or change a federal law or policy, and 60% of a state vote to add or change a state law or policy. District votes are simply the majority. This is to prevent districts and states from losing their ability to make their own laws and govern themselves. This would simplify our new Constitution and allow the different levels of government to continually evolve and adapt.

Article IV: A higher governing body will not interfere with a lower governing body unless that lower body is unable to govern itself, has asked for assistance, or is interfering with the operations of another body in a way that's deemed against the law. Once an individual, district, or state needs assistance from a higher governing body, they will lose their right to govern themselves; until such time that they are given autonomy by the higher governing body, or are able to contribute taxes at a rate equal to the national per capita average. The national population shall always be the highest governing body. This is why it would be best to have federal votes that fix nationwide problems like homelessness; as a district could make a law or policy that forces their homeless to mass migrate to another district. That would negatively affect that other district, which is against the law. The terms 'negatively affect' or 'interfere' are very vague and would need pages of appendages in order to define what that means. I'm not going to bore you with that. But it is something that would always need updating.

Article V: It will take at least ⅔ of the federal population to add, change, or remove laws in the Constitution. This would simply be tweaking the law that already exists but refers to elected officials, who will have no actual power through direct democracy. This doesn't mean ⅔ of a federal vote; it means ⅔ of the actual voting population. If ⅔ of the population wanted to change a constitutional law, then there would obviously be something wrong with that law and should be changed. But to have that many people on board with anything would be very difficult, and is what gives the Constitution its power.

We'll probably not have the numbers to change the Constitution for multiple elections – the Senate likely being the most difficult to take over. As long as we show the non-believers that this system can work, then they should jump on board, eventually. Otherwise, we'll have to wait for the young to come of age and do workarounds with bills.

The Supreme Court and the Constitution should not restrict authority over the laws that the majority of Americans want to enact, or how we want our government to function – how can that be real democracy? We need to evolve democracy to what is possible in this technological age and that means rewriting the Constitution. There will be more Articles added throughout the book that coincide with different chapters.

Remember the point of life? To always grow and get better at life – you can't do that if you don't have control of your life. In many ways, it's a harder sell than giving the power to someone else – someone who promises a safe and secure future where you don't have to make any hard decisions. Perhaps the evolution of America is still at that stage, and I'm wasting my time here. Perhaps other countries will take the lead on bringing about direct democracy – since these ideas are universal from country to country.

Switzerland already has a primitive form of mail-in direct democracy. And a county in Sweden is experimenting with it as well. Even if America is not ready for this, they will be one day. My goal is not to change American politics in the next year or two; this chapter is part of a 10-year plan. My intent is to plant a seed and hopefully it sprouts in enough people to make this happen in the future. The young are desperate for any sort of change – they can see how broken this system is and they want no part of it.

Real democracy is not going to be championed by the baby boomers, who are afraid of change and of technology. This is all about the young. It won't be long before they outnumber the old; in fact, they already do. We'll drag the elderly along, kicking and screaming...well, probably not kicking and screaming, more like moaning and drooling. Sorry, old people, I hate to make a joke on your behalf...but you have been ignoring the problems of the world for long enough. You deserve a little kick in the ass.

Chapter 2
Communication

The media we watch or read, how we talk to each other, and the information available to us by whatever means is all communication. It's the most essential ingredient to a healthy democracy. This is the shortest chapter, and the least interesting, yet it's the most important. It's short because I don't have much to add for how to better communication – capitalism is doing a fine job with that. This is all about the dangers of losing freedom of speech.

One suggestion for improvement is in regards to news networks, and a law surrounding truthful reporting. If you claim to be a 'news' source and have 'news' in your title, then you have to be able to prove that everything you're saying is a factual truth. If there are any opinions, then it should clearly say somewhere on the screen, or after each point being made, that it's only opinion and not fact. I think that would help clear up a lot of the misinformation out there that people believe to be true because their 'news source' said it to them. If there are already laws like this, then they're obviously not being enforced very well.

I also have another suggestion regarding the internet – we need to make sure everyone has easy access to it. The internet could be argued as the most important invention in human history – aside from the other inventions that make the internet possible. Forgetting about the negative side effects that it has caused in people's lives, it is crucial to fixing our world. It has essentially turned us into the type of alien race we see in movies, that is able to communicate with each other – it's the Silk Road of the 21st Century, except it now allows 6 billion people to instantly learn anything. Imagine how quickly we could improve our world if we let go of our egos and truly learned from each other – the ego of a country can be the most massive and thereby restricting to growth...cough, cough, America. I would have never been able to write this book without the internet. It's the most important tool for education, and therefore our evolution. Even the most poor and destitute individuals could come up with world changing ideas if they're given access to the internet.

Of course, the internet can be used for evil as well. And since everything must have balance, it can also be used to propel mankind into a prosperous and sustainable future. Or, it can be withheld from us by corrupt governments – I believe this path is the worst option in terms of our evolution. We need to make sure this form of communication is never restricted.

The word dictatorship gets thrown around a lot, but I wonder how often people really think about what this means. It's quite possible to have a benevolent dictator, as has happened with monarchies of the past. Unfortunately, to get into that position in this day and age requires the kind of ruthless and self-serving personality that is incredibly dangerous towards world peace. Many citizens of China are actually probably quite happy with what a dictator has done for their lives. China can get a lot done without the red tape and bureaucratic nonsense that the current, primitive democracies of the world have to go through. However, I don't think I need to tell you the dangers of letting an individual, or small group of people, have complete control over a country, or over the world. Also, under a dictatorship, the people at the bottom have almost zero chance of ever rising to the top.

Say what you will about America and its broken democracy, but you can still be born into poverty and rise to incredible heights through no one's actions but your own. To do that under a dictatorship would require you to kneel to those leaders, and they would then have to allow you to succeed. They have complete control over all aspects of every individual's life. That cannot be the path that we strive to go on, and if we continue the way we are going, then China will have that same power over much of the world.

China censors what its citizens can search online. What are they afraid of? They obviously don't want journalists reporting on corruption and human cruelty, that's pretty clear. But it really mostly comes down to a method of control. Once you're able to control people in a small way, it becomes easier to take more and more power away from them in the future.

I would say that they want to keep them ignorant and in the dark about democracy, but they allow their citizens to travel the world. Those citizens are obviously learning about how the rest of the world works. This gives them the mirage of freedom. The most troubling of it all is not being allowed to criticize their leaders. They're also not allowed to watch pornography. Now, I'm not saying that's good or bad, but it sure does explain why all they do is work! Maybe to slow them down, all we have to do is get them hooked on porn!

Where does it lead a country when their leaders can do whatever they please, and nobody can report on it? It leads to everyone at the top taking everything and no way to change it, aside from a bloody revolution. This is most definitely what's going to need to happen in countries like Russia, China, Iran, Saudi Arabia, etc., before the people can have an honest democracy. Other countries invading, trying to spread democracy, has obviously not worked in the Middle East...or Vietnam.

People need to first want democracy and then they need to fight for it. They need to earn it and appreciate it. When it's forced on a people before they're ready, then it becomes just another form of dictatorship – because the people have not set the rules, someone else has. They don't appreciate it because it was just given to them. Also, the people are unable to prevent corruption from the top – it becomes too top-heavy. On the flip side, it becomes corrupt if it stagnates and doesn't evolve, such as in America. We will create a system that makes the process of going from dictatorship to democracy a less difficult path. Of course, the infrastructure for communication throughout an entire country has to be in place first. Our global evolution towards world peace is entirely dependent on communication...and not having powerful dictators.

A dictatorship only exists because of one thing – a lack of free speech. Once you lose free speech, you lose the ability for peaceful transitions of power. We take free speech and freedom of the press for granted in the free world. But journalists are under attack, truth is under attack, and those being deceived don't even have any idea. They're all fed the same lies from the same sources, disguised as fact and news. What if we were all fed that same information with nothing else to counteract it? That doesn't seem too impossible. That's what those countries with dictatorships face.

Maybe you're an American and you're okay with what I just described. All you want out of life is safety and security – someone telling you how to think and how to spend your day. But that's not the majority – I have no facts to back this up, but if it's not true, then we're all screwed. I have to believe that the universe wants us to evolve and succeed.

Imagine a world that China owns: they own the media networks, they own whoever makes your cell phones and TVs, and they own all of the news sources. This is unlikely to happen, but it's certainly possible. You think the Chinese overlords want to own the world so they can give freedom to everyone? You think they'll all sit around talking about how wealthy they all became through this system of oppression, but now say, 'enough is enough, guys, we're going to give the world complete freedom now!' I don't think so. It's also possible that all of the richest individuals in the world, who own all of the media outlets, decide that people don't need to know certain information, and they censor what's put out there. Perhaps it's already happening. Ah, let's be honest, it's definitely happening.

One thing is certain; we, in the free world, have access to enough of the truth out there. It's impossible to say all of the truth, but certainly we learn enough to make changes. We know that this system is broken, and that's all we need to know.

If they ever take away our right to freely communicate with each other, then we've just lost democracy. They may make it seem like it's for your safety; in fact, they definitely will, but that's a lie. The only thing that will ever make you truly safe in the long term is knowing the truth.

Everything I suggest in this book must be done peacefully through the democratic process. But if they ever take away the freedom of press or free speech, then every single citizen needs to take to the streets and not leave until you get your democracy back. You're so eager to use your guns against a government that wants to oppress you? That would be the time to do so. You do not go to work, you do not listen to the authority, and you shut the system down! They are nothing without you! You're the ones that make them rich. If you stop working, they stop making money – the system collapses. You must never stop in that fight to get free speech back because it is the root of democracy. I will warn you, it will be a subtle and gradual process.

Everyone knows that they couldn't just take away free speech in America without a civil war. So, they'll do it slowly, like telling you they can spy on anything you're doing, and it's for your safety – in order to stop the terrorists, that are essentially a drop in the ocean compared to what an unhealthy lifestyle and unhealthy planet kills. Shockingly, that seems like a fair trade to many people because fear has blinded logic. Then, they'll start attacking the journalists who report on things they don't like being shared, calling it the fake news when it's quite obviously the truth. Shoot, these things sound a little familiar. Then, since they already know everything you're saying, they'll censor who sees certain types of information. Say, for instance, a certain individual was trying to start a political revolution. He or she posts on Facebook, Twitter, and Instagram all sorts of different information. It looks like it's being shared, but nobody is seeing it. Or, they just kill that individual instead. I'm not saying these things have happened, but they probably have.

The beginning steps to losing our freedom of speech have already started. We can't let it go any further. Without free-flowing communication, world peace, real democracy, and a free society will never be possible. And we might lose our free porn. Although, you wouldn't have to convince people to riot over that, so that part's probably safe.

Chapter 3
Energy and the Environment

These are my two favorite topics because they are the most important elements to a healthy and sustainable future. Energy is everything for a functioning society. When we solve the energy crisis, we solve the vast majority of problems on this planet. We'll be able to grow food anywhere without polluting the environment. We can produce as much water as we'll ever need. It completely transforms the struggle for survival, which will allow everyone to focus on the meaningful aspects of creating a fulfilling life.

The fact that clean, renewable energy isn't the number one focus of the government is probably the most criminal thing that politicians have done to us. More like it's the most harmful thing we've done to ourselves by allowing it to happen. The fact that the fossil fuel industries dictate so much legislation is the only red flag I need to say that politicians need to go. Or, at the very least, create more stringent laws that limit the amount of money corporations can give to politicians. How about no donations at all? Let's only allow publicly funded campaigns, like many other countries do, with a set amount of money that each party gets. Although, that still doesn't solve the problem that the system doesn't truly represent all of the different ideologies of people. Or, that they sit and argue instead of actually doing what needs to be done. Or, that they're afraid to tackle difficult problems because of the optics during the next election. But I digress.

Clean renewable energy is going to have to largely replace fossil fuels if we're going to save our home – the planet. But these energy sources are intermittent and unreliable. Therefore, storing this energy is the most important problem to solve. Unfortunately, batteries are likely not the solution to this storage problem – they're the VHS of energy. To mine the amount of lithium it would take to power the world would be very harmful to the planet, not to mention unsustainable. The cost to recycle lithium batteries costs more than actually just producing them from scratch – which will very likely change. It's also not a viable option for the industries that need new fuel sources the most: jet aircraft, trains, ships, buses, and the trucking industry. However, it's unlikely that jets will ever get off of fossil fuels until a trans-formative energy is invented. Or, perhaps Elon Musk's goal of building frictionless tubes around the world will become a reality, and eliminate the need for jet aircraft. Regardless, we're going to need clean sources of energy, and we need to figure out how to store that energy.

Hydrogen is the most abundant element in the universe. For those of you that don't know how a hydrogen fuel cell works, I'll give you a simple explanation. When you combine hydrogen gas and air, they form water and heat. This process creates electricity through a proton exchange membrane (more complicated than you need to know).

We can collect hydrogen by running an electrical current through water that has two different metal plates immersed in it (typically made from iron, which is one of the most abundant metals on this planet). One plate collects hydrogen and the other collects oxygen. They typically have to do this with fresh water because saltwater corrodes the plates too quickly. But with the amount of water you would have to use, to create the amount of hydrogen that the world would need, it's likely not feasible with freshwater.

Fairly recently, someone has discovered that you can coat the metal plates with a protective sealant that makes the plate last 1000 times longer in saltwater, which puts it almost on par with using freshwater. Now, I don't think I need to tell you that there's a lot of saltwater out there – literally all the hydrogen we'll ever need, especially since the hydrogen joins with oxygen to form water again.

The question then becomes, where do you get that energy to separate the hydrogen and the oxygen in the first place? That's where wind, solar, geothermal, tidal and wave energy come in. You don't need batteries to harness this energy – you only need batteries to transport and store that energy. But batteries are bad for the environment and need continual replacement, again, bad for the environment. Plus, they're just not feasible for the transport industry that can't afford to sit around and wait for their vehicles to charge to go another 300 miles. It's possible that they completely transform what a battery is made of, and make it ultra light and environmentally friendly – that would be a great solution. Even if that happens, Hydrogen still has other uses and investment into this industry will pay itself off in many ways.

Hydrogen is transportable and refillable; although, these steps are more complicated than with fossil fuels. We can harvest hydrogen where renewable energies from solar, wind and the ocean are abundant. And then transport the hydrogen to filling stations, like your local gas station or power grids. This could be a solution to an energy source for a lot of the transportation industry until cold fusion becomes the standard, and it will. They're already able to create cold fusion but it takes an incredible amount of energy to start the process, it isn't producing a lot of energy, and the machine it takes to do it is the size of a house. They'll figure it out but it's going to take some time, and we can't rely purely on oil, gas, and coal until that happens.

A problem with renewable energy is the materials and fossil fuels it will take to turn these sources into our main energy suppliers. We'll get more into that in the next chapter. There are also problems with hydrogen, as it's a highly explosive element – this is one argument that the oil and gas industries will often use to try and suppress innovation. Gas can be explosive too, but they've built gas tanks to prevent that. They can do the same with hydrogen, it would just take more shielding and safeguards. It's also difficult to compress and transport efficiently – it would likely be most viable for places with lots of room for storage and abundant renewable energy.

We could build giant storage tanks underground, with the renewable energy plants on top of them. Those storage tanks should need zero maintenance and last until cold fusion is mastered. The technology for storing hydrogen is getting better every day – anything is possible if the will is there. The will to get off oil has just not been there until very recently. Since the government moves slower than a glacier in getting anything done, we need to step in and do it ourselves.

Some will say that capitalism will dictate the pace that new energies evolve, but I say that capitalism doesn't take into account the health and long-term costs to our planet. It only cares about profit in the foreseeable future. We need more of a balance than that.

The oil and gas industries have a stranglehold on energy production. Without government investment and legislation, it could take decades before another energy source, that isn't a battery, could compete. That's not acceptable. We can't be burning hydrocarbons, that come from the ground, at this rate, and the rate will only keep going up as more developing countries get out of poverty. Perhaps it's already too late, and we'll have to figure out ways to get the carbon out of the atmosphere...not perhaps, definitely. Thankfully, there are already carbon recapturing plants that can do this.

There is also a ground-breaking process being developed in which we put olivine (a mineral found in basalt rocks) on beaches. This mineral reacts with water and sunshine and forms rocks that store C02, that then sit on the ocean floor for millions of years – this process only takes a couple of years. It's also a very abundant mineral, and would only take 0.14% of the earth's shorelines to offset global emissions. I believe this is our best option for quickly eliminating C02 from the atmosphere.

You may say that we could never get off of fossil fuels quickly enough to stop the catastrophes that are bound to happen. And that is a fair point. But get this, there is a simple process of combining hydrogen gas with waste carbon emissions that creates synthetic fuel – as in jet fuel and the very gasoline that goes in your vehicle. Those carbon recapturing plants I just mentioned are already doing this, and they are creating fuel at a cost of $4/gallon, which is only going to keep going down. It's also a much cleaner fuel because it doesn't have nitrogen or sulfur in it. Therefore, we need to be trapping all emissions from factories that depend on fossil fuels in their manufacturing process, and turn the carbon waste into synthetic fuel. We would also need to recycle the other gas emissions, like nitrous oxide and sulfur dioxide.

We will need to be creating synthetic fossil fuels for many decades. To immediately replace all of the cars on the road with electric cars would do way more harm than good. You may think you're helping the environment by buying an electric car, but the environmental damage created from building that new car outweighs the environmental impact from just using your gasoline powered car until its end of life.

To help with this, we need to invest heavily into replacing all fossil fuel energy plants into renewable energy plants – using hydrogen as the energy storage. We should also be creating hydrogen from nuclear power plants, using the excess heat generated. But we need to be phasing out nuclear power – the storage of nuclear waste is something that future generations are going to have a difficult time with, and that's not fair to them. Plus, the American people are paying for nuclear waste storage and disposal with their taxes. It costs us billions of dollars a year and that's only going to keep going up. But while those nuclear plants are functioning, we might as well use all excess energy they create to build our renewable energy plants. The same goes for hydro-electric power plants.

Even if we use these excess energy sources, a lot of fossil fuel derived energy will be needed in order to create a completely green planet. We should trap those gases and turn the carbon back into fuel. We can recycle fossil fuels, many times over, we simply have to create legislation and invest in the process. Eventually, we'll be able to create a system where we're only using synthetic fossil fuels in jet aircraft and necessary industrial processes, but it's carbon-neutral because it's coming from a renewable source.

In order to do that, we would need to create bio-plastics from biological sources like hemp, seaweed, trees or bamboo, and then burn those plastics for energy instead of recycling them, which would be better for the environment as long as we trapped all gases being created. We collect the carbon dioxide from burning those bio-plastics and make synthetic fuels. The plants regrow and collect the same amount of carbon that's released from burning the synthetic fuel. It's a carbon-neutral process that creates energy, fuel and plastics; all from growing plants and collecting hydrogen through renewable energy sources. Plastics that need to last a long time will still have to be made with fossil fuels, and those that require a short shelf life should be made with renewable sources. Most importantly, we need to use less plastics. People drink bottled water, instead of filtering their own, and tell themselves that they're not hurting the environment because they're recycling the bottle – that's simply not correct. And if you're not even recycling that bottle, then you're just a horrible human being – sorry, but it's true. Plastic is obviously an incredible material that we use for a ridiculous amount of purposes, but we're going to pay the price down the road if we don't become more responsible with this dangerous material.

We could also have a fleet of ships collecting plastic from the oceans, burning those plastics to power the ships, and collecting all gases that are produced in order to create synthetic fuels. It would be easy enough to convert, or build 10 vessels that have a large boiler to burn plastic that powers turbines, tanks and a compressor to store those emissions, and mechanisms to scoop plastic from the ocean. They then transfer that carbon to a hydrogen plant, where they synthesize fuel. Can you imagine renewable energy plants creating synthetic fuels and that's the only place where we get petrol from? We could have factories recycling gasoline in the middle of a city. It's possible, it would just take an incredible investment...we'll get to that.

We simply can't just leave all of that plastic in the ocean. Since fossil fuels were already used to create that plastic, we might as well turn it back into fuel. The Pacific Ocean Garbage Patch is twice the size of Texas. I have a hard time believing that individuals threw enough plastic in the ocean to create that. Not to mention, most of the materials in that patch are plastics that normal people would never go near an ocean with. I think it's quite possible that some container ships we send to Asia, with our plastics and trash, dump their loads in the ocean. Most of Asia seems to care very little about the environment, would rather not even receive these 'recyclables' in the first place, and the transport companies get paid either way – where is the incentive to deliver this stuff? Even if they did deliver it all, a very small percentage of what we think is being recycled actually gets recycled, which is why it would be better to simply burn it, trap those gases and make synthetic fuels. We can do this endlessly – the only limiting factor is having enough hydrogen gas. Obtaining the clean energy to create enough hydrogen will always be the limiting factor here. We can solve that with government investment. And it's going to take some time.

I think it's North America's responsibility to clean up the Pacific Garbage Patch. With the process I just described, I believe it could pay for itself, through the sale of synthetic fuel, while also creating jobs. By my rough calculations, it should take 10 ships, that never stop, under 15 years to clean up this area of garbage. We should be focusing on these sorts of industries – those that help the environment, create jobs, and pay for itself. Most projects that reverse damage that we've done to the environment will not be profitable. That's the reason why nobody focuses on these tasks – nobody at the top stands to make a profit. We can fix that faulty system.

There are many other ways to create carbon-neutral energy. Humans have genetically modified a tree, the hybrid poplar, to grow to harvest size in about 5 years. They grow in rows and even regrow in their own stumps, which makes replanting a simple procedure. What I don't think some people realize is that wood burning is a carbon-neutral process – as long as you replant what you've cut down. A tree that is burned for energy releases the exact same amount of carbon that the tree reabsorbs when it grows back to its original size. We can also collect the carbon emissions and create synthetic fuels to help subsidize the cost. It's also a sustainable resource.

What we can't do is cut down forests that already exist and use wood that has been growing for decades – that would take too long to be carbon-neutral and also destroys the beauty of our natural world. There are plenty of areas where we could grow millions of acres of hybrid poplar, eucalyptus or willow where the natural world is already gone – like in areas after a forest fire.

So, why do energy companies burn coal instead of commercially grown trees? Because coal produces about 30% more heat per pound than renewable sources. When the bottom line is all that matters, that 30% becomes a pretty big deal. When the environment and sustainability come into the equation, that 30% becomes meaningless. A problem also exists with hybrid-poplars and disease, but we should be able to solve that. Also, it would not be possible to power America through bio-fuels alone. There's also the issue with fertilizer, which we'll get to in the next chapter. This process should mostly be geared towards creating carbon-neutral, synthetic fuels. As I said, we are going to need hydrocarbon fuels for a long time, and these bio-fuel plants could be where we create a carbon-neutral source.

When I was in grade school, I remember my teacher saying to us, 'if you build a perpetual motion machine, you'll be the richest person in the world.' I immediately thought, 'why not use the magnetism of the planet?' The thought went away because I didn't even know what I was thinking, as I was just a stupid kid. Recently, I've watched countless videos of people creating just that – a perpetual motion machine powering a light bulb off of the earth's magnetic field. However, this process is also highly unlikely to produce the energy needs of America. It should spark your imagination to the possibilities, though.

I've also seen videos of people running motorbikes with polluted water, using the same process I described earlier with hydrogen – except now I realize that they would have had to have been charging a battery from a different source, to make up for the loss in energy it takes to separate the hydrogen. Still, if all you had to do was charge one battery, that would power your car using polluted river water, then I'd say that's a pretty good trade-off.

This bike was pumping hydrogen gas directly into a carburetor and combustion engine. I've read this is possible, but hydrogen has less energy than hydrocarbons (fossil fuels) and would likely only power something small; unless there was a turbocharger installed. I don't suggest this as a solution as this process creates nitrous oxide, which is no good. We could solve that problem as well, though, by using pure oxygen in the combustion process (instead of air, which has nitrogen in it).

There are desert cities around the world that have done something really quite simple, yet remarkable. They use hundreds of mirrors that move with the sun and direct the sunlight into one concentrated area. That area heats to over 2000 degrees and boils water, which turns a turbine and powers small cities. Besides cleaning the mirrors, very little maintenance is involved. As for the replacement cost, that's pretty low as well because mirrors last a very long time. We could use hydrogen to store energy for when the sun isn't shining, and to heat the water back up before the sun starts doing its thing. The hydrogen storage tanks could be directly underneath the mirrors and take up no extra room. If we build pipes that bring ocean water to the deserts of the world, then we could create all the hydrogen we would ever need – as well as supply the desert with freshwater and allow for farming.

There are tons of different ways to create cheap, clean, and renewable energy. It isn't going to be just one source, until cold fusion takes over, that powers cities – we're going to need to use many different sources of energy. Not to mention, homes are mostly going to need to power themselves – we'll get to that. We're also going to need to charge high energy users more money, in order to promote responsible energy use. There should be a base energy consumption that a responsible person or family would normally use, and anything over that would be charged at a premium. Saving the environment isn't just about energy, though.

We produce an incredible amount of waste. Back in the day, companies used to build products to last, because they got business through word of mouth. These days, people have learned that they can produce products that break after a short amount of time, and make more money. I used to live on an air mattress...struggling artist and all. It would get holes in it after a very short time. I would find the leaks and it would be pretty obvious that they had created weak points in the rubber where air would escape after just a couple of months. Products like this can't be recycled and create a large amount of garbage that go into landfills. The company pays nothing for this.

We have to create a garbage tax to incentivize companies to build products that last. For every extra year that they're able to give a warranty, the tax is reduced. We could also reduce the tax if they use recycled materials, and is recyclable itself. There are many different areas where we could be creating balance between capitalism and the environment. Right now, immediate profit is the only concern, and the people, not the corporations, are going to end up paying the balance in the future.

We also throw away most of our electronics. The materials in these products are toxic for the environment when they end up in landfills. They're also expensive to mine. Not to mention, we depend on China to mine those materials for us, which is simply unacceptable going forward. We need to charge a deposit on all electronics, like we do with cans and bottles, in order to incentivize people to recycle these products. The cost to recycle them should also be added onto the production costs; recycling these rare earth minerals actually costs more than producing them from scratch. But we need to recycle these materials because they're toxic and in limited supply. The added cost onto consumers shouldn't be that much to simply break even on this process.

It's going to take serious legislation to fix our environment. Unfortunately, not everyone feels the same way about our ecosystem. Some only care about it if it affects their health, or if it limits the amount of money they can make because of legislation. I care about the environment because the natural world energizes me. The earth has almost 8 billion people – there is no other animal, besides insects, that even comes close to that number. I would lie if I said that I cared about a human life more than the life of an animal that's critically endangered, because I don't. But you need to fix human society if you want to fix the natural world.

In reality, nothing we do really matters in the grand scheme of things – the sun and the earth will go on, with or without us. Life will rebound after we've completely destroyed the planet, with or without us. But that is such a lazy path to take, and I refuse to take it. It doesn't mean I don't care about the economy or human health, it's quite the opposite – those are the most important aspects to creating a happy and sustainable society. But we need a healthy planet with a naturally functioning ecosystem to create true sustainability – one in which we're not constantly fighting nature.

If the entire planet was all concrete and zoos, then we would lose what makes the earth such an amazing place to live in. We're already losing it at unprecedented rates. One would think that this should be a priority of the people, especially in an advanced society like America, but it's pretty clear that the economy is king.

Trump put the environment at the bottom of the 'give a shit' list. Why would he care? He's a selfish old man that can see the end of the road. If the natural world is gone in 50 years, then so what? What's shocking is that his followers don't seem to care either. Is that because they've never traveled somewhere untouched by man? If they've left their state, it's probably only to go to a neighboring state. Or the big trip to Florida, California, or all-inclusive Mexico. Maybe it's just too out of their bubble to relate to, or care about, the destruction of the natural world. This is odd, given that fresh drinking water has become such a hot topic in so many American communities. Non-polluted rivers and lakes equal clean, fresh drinking water...that's the easiest math problem we're going to do in this book.

I would suggest they don't care because these people are in survival mode. They don't have room in their hearts or minds for the environment when they're struggling to survive themselves. Take Asia, or Africa, for example, the people are so poor that they're willing to poach the last of their beautiful animals in order to feed their families for just a couple of months. Most of Asia has already decimated their oceans from over-fishing in their struggle to survive. They're destroying apex predator species like whales, dolphins and sharks, which upsets the entire ecosystem. The oceans do not exist in a bubble – what they do to their oceans in Asia affects the oceans around the world. I'm all for freedom of action, until it negatively affects other life on this planet. They need to be stopped. But you can't stop them with force, there has to be an incentive for them to do it themselves. We'll get to that, of course.

The problem with this theory of Trump supporters not caring because they're in survival mode is that many of his supporters are middle to upper-class white Americans. It's simply about greed for them...also religion and immigration. They don't want legislation that affects how much money they can make – the environment be damned. They simply refuse to believe they're doing any harm because their greed and comfort has blinded them. And change scares them. Those who seek the truth and don't fear change are going to have to be the majority, or we're in for a very rough future.

Perhaps people have already invented world-changing technologies, and the oil industry has shut them up. It's certainly possible, and there are plenty of conspiracy theories out there that suggest this. Let's not live in the past; let's focus on fixing our future. In order to do that quickly, we have to take power away from these people, and not leave it up to capitalism – which cares nothing about our long-term survival.

We're going to have to invest heavily in renewable energy plants, hydrogen plants, synthetic fuel plants, and farms that can create bio-plastics. As well as give interest-free loans to individuals to create their own renewable energy sources on their homes. As long as these industries can at least be profit neutral, and employ millions of people that pay taxes, then the investment will pay itself off. It will take time, but we should be able to get to a carbon-neutral stage while still using petrol. We must have an end goal in sight, instead of just living from election to election with no long-term plan.

I believe that energy is a right of the people and should not be in capitalism. But without capitalism, the drive for innovation dies as well. Some people may have that intrinsic drive to just do something good for the world, but most people do it to be rich. I think that aspect doesn't need to change when it comes to energy innovation. You do this through patents. China, by the way, has ridiculous patent laws which allow their citizens to steal patents from other countries and produce it themselves. This is one thing I will commend Trump on for battling. However, come to think of it, what did he really do? What change, besides war, destruction, and wasteful spending on symptoms have any politicians really done in the last 50 years? Granted, China has the world bent over a barrel right now, because of their non-existent environmental laws and what they're able to mine at a low cost because of that. We're getting products for cheap, but the balance always has to be paid in some form. We're paying that price with environmental destruction and by allowing a ruthless dictator to take over the world.

With the patent, a person, or organization develops a ground-breaking way to make energy. They then convince the government, which is now run by the people, to adopt this new form of energy creation. Those inventors should get, in perpetuity, a small percentage of what it costs to produce this technology. If it costs 100 billion dollars to produce machines, say for cold fusion to power America, and that person makes 5% on the energy patent, then they would make 5 billion dollars. The people would pay 5% extra, on top of production costs, to pay the owner of this patent. The people then just pay the cost of producing the energy after that, no profit made by any middlemen – besides the incentives going towards production quotas.

I feel like 5% would still create the drive needed for energy innovation, especially when it comes to long-term global usage (which is what inventors should be focusing on). It could be 10% or 15% – whatever seems fair and decided upon by the people. We must always keep in mind that inventors and their investors need to have an incentive, or we become too socialist, and innovation dies.

America can and will create clean, renewable energy. But how do we do that for the developing world? Each year the developed world gives billions of dollars to Africa and poor countries in Asia for basic necessities. It gives them fish instead of teaching them how to fish...or better yet, giving them fish farms so they can feed themselves. I'm not implying we give them actual fish farms because I used to be a diver for fish farms, and it's a horrific industry for the environment – unless we build inland fish farms using renewable energy. Instead, I'm suggesting we build hydrogen and synthetic fuel plants on the coasts of Africa.

Africa has an incredible amount of renewable energy with the sun and coastlines. They could have an innovative industry to call their own. An industry with no profits taken by greedy corporations, but strict adherence to rules must be followed so as to prevent corruption in those countries. All of the profits they receive would have to go to the people of Africa, with incentives for those running the plants to meet production quotas. There always has to be an incentive, or they become as useless and inefficient as the government. I'll probably say that a few more times in this book to really drill it into your heads.

The money that these hydrogen and fuel plants produce could build schools, farms, and infrastructure – but where I think a lot of it needs to go is into freshwater production. They need to desalinate ocean water and replenish their groundwater so that they can farm around the entire continent. Replenishing aquifers is not a difficult thing, but it takes time, and they need to get on it immediately. Desalinated water lacks nutrients and tastes bad, but once it filters through the spongy layer and into the ground reservoirs, it collects nutrients, and the carbon in the ground filters out the nasty taste.

They can then use this water throughout the entire continent by building wells. They would need thousands of these desalination and groundwater replacement plants, but that works out pretty well for a continent that needs job creation. The developed world needs to be investing in Africa and these industries. Unfortunately, the haves don't seem too concerned with helping the have-nots. That's really unfortunate because as a global village, we can only rise as high as our weakest member. We must all rise up together if we're to attain world peace.

A lot of the goals I've set for myself revolve around fixing Africa. Asian countries mostly have the infrastructure and money to fix themselves, they just need to end corruption – and that's for the people to do. And, honestly, Asia is too big of a problem for me to take on immediately. In my opinion, that continent is the greatest danger to a sustainable and healthy society, simply because they've overpopulated past any sort of fixable level. I'll talk about what I think needs to be done in regards to overpopulation later.

I believe Africa has the most beautiful natural world on planet earth, and they're destroying it for survival. Asia, mainly China, plays a large part in that because they're the ones buying the horns and whatever else from these majestic creatures, for God only knows what ridiculous purpose. China is a huge problem to be tackled in creating a healthy and sustainable planet, have I mentioned that? But Africa is ripe for the fixing, and I am going to dedicate everything I have to help create a sustainable continent.

The most efficient way to save the animals in those countries is to create tourist hot spots – a lot of people want to see those animals up close and in the wild. African wildlife is only going to survive with the help of capitalism – it has to be more profitable to keep them alive than to allow individuals to poach them. That can be done through tourism. It's such a beautiful continent, why wouldn't you want to go there?

Well, first of all, those safari trips cost a fortune – so let's create a ton of them and lower the cost. Second of all, most of Africa is not really ready for tourism. They need a lot of help with infrastructure and taking care of those...shoot, what are they called? Oh right, those genocidal warmongers that kidnap small children and force them to murder other warmongers. What Africa needs is money, industry, and hope for a better future. The people will take care of the rest once their basic survival needs are met. Humans are, after all, the most impressive species this planet has ever seen.

You may ask how all of these ideas regarding energy can take off. In the developed world, governments need to be heavily investing in these industries. By the end of the book, you'll see how we can make that possible without collapsing the economy. As for Africa, I plan to hopefully jump-start that process.

I'm first and foremost a screenwriter. I recently got the green-light to direct my first movie, and then COVID-19 happened (just so you know, I'm writing this book while in quarantine). We'll hopefully continue our plans once this is all over. The movie is a comedy called NO POLITICS, and it's about American politics – big stretch, I know. I have many different scripts that all voice different ways to change the world. What really excites me is business. I've never cared much for money, besides having enough to live on; I've only ever cared about new experiences and learning new things.

However, all of my focus and energy is now going into making money. I have ideas on how to make billions to put into Africa and these renewable energy plants. I don't want any of those profits; I want it all to go to Africa so that they can fix the mess we've put them in. I'm not going to get into the details of my plans in this chapter – rest assured that I have solid ideas on how to make this happen. All of my plans depend on you, the people of the world, getting behind these ideas and supporting what I do. You can do this by buying the products I invest in, watching the movies I produce, and reading the books I write. Without you, I can't do anything. We'll talk more about your role at the end; trust me, it's an easy job you have.

As far as the environment in the free world goes, it's really not a concern of mine. There are plenty of problems and ambivalence by our leaders, but for the most part it's not a pressing concern; which could be why Trump supporters don't care about it. California is running out of groundwater, but I've already talked about how to fix that, and they will – they have the infrastructure to do it.

America is one of the largest carbon polluters on the planet, but we can easily fix that while creating jobs and strengthening our economy – an economy where the majority of wealth isn't going to the top 10%. Ocean levels are rising and cities are sinking, which is going to cost trillions of dollars to replace coastal cities. But I believe human ingenuity will figure out how to solve these problems in the developed world.

The developing world is going to be hit the hardest, and in their struggle to survive they're going to destroy their natural world. That is my concern when it comes to the environment. Another major concern is the health of the oceans – which take in a large amount of carbon dioxide and produce the oxygen we breathe. They also produce a lot of the food that we eat. Dead oceans result in a struggling population. Let's work on preventing that, shall we?

The real problem I'm focusing on in the developed world is the inaction of the government to do anything until shit has really hit the fan, and they have no other choice but to do some work. So, let's first fix the system, make it more efficient and accountable, and the rest of the problems in the free world fall into place. Once good ideas can be acted on quickly, instead of being held up in Congress for months to then just be ignored, then we can start fixing the problems in America.

My first goal with America is to get the idea of direct democracy into the mainstream. If Americans choose to continue with ambivalence and inaction, with the economy and the immediate future as the only concern (eating the one cookie), then I'm building a bunker and waiting for the apocalypse. Please don't make me do that. Especially since the internet and free porn would be lost too. I can't live in a bunker without a constant supply of free porn. You know what I'm talking about, pervert.

Chapter 4
Food and Resources

Who here thinks food is important, please raise your hands? Okay, I can't see you, and you probably didn't raise your hand, but I know you think food is important. Food, water, shelter and air: the most important elements for human survival. Without every single individual having these needs met, they will struggle and never evolve past the animal stage. When humans are behaving like wild animals, we'll never have world peace. Everyone needs their basic requirements met. After we've solved the energy crisis, this will become quite an easy thing to accomplish. Until that time, I have some ideas.

Perhaps you don't know much about food production. You've kept the blinders on because you've got enough problems to worry about. Or, maybe you've just never been interested or exposed to it. Trust me when I tell you, it's a complete disaster. The typical farmer has been replaced by giant corporations. And what do you think giant corporations care about? Sustainability and your well-being! Wait, that doesn't sound right. Money, that's what I was thinking, money! They don't care if they destroy the land they're using, at least they don't seem to care, which seems odd. They just want to make as much as they can as quickly as possible and retire – leave the problems for the next guy.

A plant, not unlike the human body, has everything it needs to fight off disease, pests, and infection, when healthy. When unhealthy, not unlike humans, they need all sorts of drugs and pesticides to stay alive – I guess most humans don't ingest pesticides, but you get the idea. Organic farming has become a big industry because people don't want these pesticides in their bodies. I'm not sure if the environment is their major concern since organic farms use pesticides as well. These farms simply use pesticides that are deemed natural, like copper. But copper is not so great for the environment, especially in the quantities that they sometimes dump it in. The fact of the matter is that money has ruined the farming industry, including organic.

At least the soil on organic farms is alive. Most of the soil that these giant, non-organic mono-crops now grow in is dead. Just to be clear, a mono-crop is a farm that grows only one type of plant, say wheat or soy, and that's it. The soil on these farms no longer has living organisms to fix the nitrogen that the plants absorb (fixing means the bacteria and other organisms turn organic matter into something the roots can absorb). So, these farms use inorganic fertilizers, and they drench their farms in nitrogen, phosphorous, and potassium. These fertilizers, especially the phosphorous, run into streams and rivers because the soil can no longer hold onto water. This runoff creates plankton blooms, which destroy life in oceans and lakes. These blooms are also created by detergents that we pour down our drains, and this needs to stop immediately. We do this by recycling all water and sewage coming from homes and never dump it into the environment.

Funny story about plankton blooms: I used to dive on fish farms. Often, plankton blooms would come along and kill just about all of the fish in the pens. Then we, as divers, would spend weeks collecting the tens of thousands of dead fish that had all been decaying at the bottom of the nets. I guess that wasn't really a funny story. Needless to say, these inorganic fertilizers are not good for the soil, and they're not good for any other part of the environment. They're also created from fossil fuels, which is unsustainable. But they're necessary because the soil is dead. Isn't learning fun?

The good news is we can create new soil. You take fish remains and wood, they do some sort of inter-species lovemaking, the really kinky kind, and they produce fertile soil. Perfect, we can do that in large quantities – both of those things are renewable resources and just take energy and the will to do it. The bad news is that these giant corporations don't care about healthy soil, rivers, lakes, or oceans. You already know what they care about, you clever devil. So, they need to be forced to care. Better yet, just go away, we'll grow the food ourselves. You've had your chance and you screwed it up. My next suggestion is going to be a bit radical.

I suggest food production be taken out of capitalism. Something so necessary and precious doesn't belong in the hands of greedy, soulless corporations. During the COVID-19 pandemic, they've talked about shutting farms down because they're no longer profitable. What then? They're also throwing food out while people starve. This industry is too important to belong to capitalism. I would say we just need to change our laws to protect the environment and grow healthier food, but it's too late for that. For those corporations to change their entire practices, and then still make money off of it, would drive our food costs to exorbitant prices. Profit needs to be taken out of food production and I'll tell you how.

In many countries around the world, kids get out of high school and do a year of government service. For most of them, especially the boys, this means military service. Now, we haven't gotten to the military chapter yet, but I think I've already mentioned how I feel about military spending in this age of economic warfare. What if, instead, these 18-year-olds went to the millions of smaller, sustainable farms that we could create in America? They would learn how to grow food, a skill everyone should know, and they would be the checks and balances for what's actually happening – since they would be eating that food as well.

You may ask, what is a sustainable farm? What's the difference if they can sustain the growth of food with inorganic fertilizers? First of all, I already talked about the plankton blooms and the runoff of fertilizers. Second of all, the plants are simply not healthy. They lack essential nutrients and will always need pesticides. Not to mention the livestock industry, which is a hundred times worse.

These giant livestock farms torture animals, like putting gestating pigs in cages where they can't even scratch themselves and go insane, all to save a few cents a pound. They line up animals in slaughterhouses where their fear hormones are then ingested into us. Ever wonder why there's such a culture of fear in America? Those hormones we're ingesting daily might have something to do with it. They're fed corn, grains, and soy, which are not their natural diets, and they're cramped together – so they're pretty much sick all of the time. How do they solve that? They pump them full of antibiotics. These slaughterhouses and processing/packaging plants have a monopoly, and are owned by very few individuals (even foreign corporations). They dictate prices and control our entire food supply. Does that sound like a secure, healthy, and sustainable practice to you? A humane practice?

We also subsidize the corn and soy industries with billions of dollars every year to produce a cheap meal that livestock shouldn't even be eating. Know what else they do with the corn? They create corn syrup that goes into most sugary things you eat and drink, and essentially the major cause of obesity and diabetes. Funny cycle: taxpayer pays the corn industry to poison them and their livestock, giant corporations growing corn make a bunch of money subsidized by your tax dollars and run to the bank, and then the taxpayers pay for all the sick people who have been eating garbage their whole lives. Shoot, was that not funny again?

A sustainable farm is actually a pretty simple concept, and there are plenty of farmers in America who are doing it now – they should be allowed to continue, as long as they can compete with the low-cost food that society should be able to create.

These farmers gave up the easy payday and didn't lease their land to corporations to destroy, and are barely making a livable income. But that more has to do with legislation that is trying to kill the small farmer than it does to their actual ability to make money. The cost for a small farmer to take their animals to inhumane slaughterhouses cuts into all of their profits. Instead, they could slaughter and butcher their animals on their land, and ship to stores nearby. They're not allowed to do that. They have to go to slaughterhouses.

This is because of safety – as in they don't want meat getting salmonella and E. coli. Because that isn't already happening in slaughterhouses, right? There's simply no possible way to create and enforce legislation that allows these farmers to slaughter their own animals, I guess. Well, I'm sure there is, but it would create work for politicians. And they would have to stop taking money from giant agri-corporations. Don't bother them, they're busy trying to get re-elected by making as little splash as possible.

My father was a sick man. He was in a motorcycle accident in his late teens and used crutches his whole life. He also had an open staph infection in his hip that never closed up, for which he would have to change the bandages daily. He wasn't a big meat eater, because whenever he would eat meat from a grocery store, it would make his infection have a big party. So, eating healthy was the only way he could survive. He was a direct barometer on how healthy certain foods were.

He used to have a farmer that had a specific way of killing his cattle, so as not to stress them out. Every day he would go out into his field and shoot his rifle among the cows. In the beginning, they would scuttle about and become agitated. After a week or two of this, they didn't even notice he was shooting a gun. Then, when he had to slaughter an animal, he would go out there and shoot one in the head.

The other cattle never had any idea. No stress hormones and no torturing of cattle in tiny pens. These were grass-fed cows (along with other supplemental feed), with enough room to graze, and this guy was making a decent living off of it. My dad could eat this meat without his infection having an orgy. Then, laws came in that didn't allow farmers to kill their own cattle. They could use slaughterhouses only, and he couldn't eat those healthy cows anymore. The farmer stopped farming because it was no longer profitable. Now, we're left with an unsustainable industry that's killing us, killing the planet, and torturing livestock in the process.

America should not raise livestock for the purpose of export. Livestock is incredibly harmful to the environment, and it's not the kind of export industry that America needs. Not to mention, these cattle are eating subsidized feed, which taxpayers pay for. These livestock farmers are not putting enough taxes back into the system to make up for all of this. Most importantly, America exports the same amount of beef that it imports – how does that make any sense? There's no reason to promote the export of such an all-around unhealthy industry.

That brings us to a very touchy subject – Americans need to eat less meat. We're not going to be able to force Americans to eat less meat, but it should be a bit more expensive, to account for livestock living in a humane environment. It's unhealthy for the environment, unhealthy for humans, and we're torturing the animals. I believe that these 18-year-olds will naturally start to eat less meat when they become a part of the slaughtering process. That's what I predict, anyway. Then again, meat will be produced in labs in the not too distant future, so everything I just said may be wasted energy.

A sustainable farm all comes down to grass management. The sun and the grass provide everything a farm needs. The animals eat the grass and provide fertilizer for the crops. What a wonderfully natural process the whole thing is. Instead of growing just one crop, they grow many different kinds of crops. These crops complement each other, and they rotate legumes into the soil every 2 or 3 years – legumes fix the nitrogen in the soil and keep it healthy, indefinitely. I would personally add my own step into these farms, such as growing trees to fuel a boiler that could power all of the farm equipment that these kids would use. Part of their job is to grow the trees and cut them down.

We could also build inland fish farms where renewable energy is abundant. We could have insect farms, black soldier fly being a good option, and feed the larvae all of the organic waste from livestock and plants (from both farms and homes). It needs to become illegal to throw out food waste because this material goes into landfills, where it is buried underneath garbage and the anaerobic conditions create methane, which is one of the worst greenhouse gases. We should pick this material up free of charge and that cost should be offset through the sale of fertilizer and feed.

The insect frass (manure) works as a great fertilizer, especially when mixed with inorganic fertilizers, because it has chitin, which gives plants a natural defense against pests – no more pesticides needed. The adult insects then get fed to the fish. We would also have to mix omega-3 fatty acids, from a sustainable source like seaweed, with this insect protein in order to raise healthy fish for consumption. The wastewater from the freshwater farms could be pumped directly into hydroponic farming systems, in which the fish manure would be the only fertilizer needed. The plants filter the water which then goes back to the fish farm. The processed fish remains are then used to create new soil. The adult flies could also be fed to chickens.

It's not just fish and insect manure that we could use – our sewage is a resource that we are spending money on instead of profiting from. Raw sewage is not suitable for edible plants because it has toxins in it, but we could use it as fertilizer for bio-fuels or industries like cotton farms. Imagine bio-fuel farms growing all around sewage plants, which would allow us to create synthetic fuel simply from our sewage and the sunshine. If we used this fertilizer to grow cotton trees, then it wouldn't be a problem as long as you don't eat your underwear. There are so many closed-loop systems like this we could be using in different industries, and we're not; because the environment is not a strong consideration for politicians or the corporations that control them.

We could create giant seaweed farms in 'dead' areas of the ocean. The benefits of doing this would be numerous, but the carbon these plants would recapture would be worth it in itself. There is a process in which seaweed is planted on a platform and suspended 50 feet below the surface. A pump transports nutrient-rich water from the depths to the surface, which then cycles back down to the depths, all from the power of wave action. Imagine thousands of farmers going into ocean areas that were previously devoid of life and farming seaweed. This is one type of farm that actually helps the environment. There is no fertilizer needed and kelp grows 3 feet a day. They would only need to harvest the top 3 feet and leave all of that flourishing sea life underneath in the kelp forests.

Seaweed has a ridiculous amount of uses, and these farmers would just need to pay for their own wage to make this an incredibly profitable investment for society.

Unfortunately, fixing our farming industry is going to be difficult, no question. We can buy the land off of polluting corporations through the power of eminent domain, or simply take it in penalty for poisoning the planet. I don't really care what the people decide to do, but once we have control of the government, we can do whatever we please. That's kind of a scary prospect. But when it comes to the purposeful destruction of farmland and human health, I think anything goes to correct that imbalance. We'd have to be careful to not treat all industries like this, but Monsanto and other giant agri-corporations? Screw them! They absolutely know what they've been doing!

Considering the land is worthless and will take time to get the soil fertile again, I would suggest not even buying the land. Simply make non-organic, for-profit farming illegal. If there's one thing America has, it's plenty of land that could be cultivated for farming. It would take time, and the transition process would certainly need planning, but it can be done.

Perhaps some of these corporations would decide to take up sustainable farming. However, that would take years and a lot of resources to accomplish, just to make very little profit. So, they're not going to do that. Since inorganic, for-profit farming is now illegal, and we're taxing the hell out of farmland that's not being used, they'll just want to get rid of the land. Then, the people can continue using those farms for the few years it will take to get sustainable farms going across the country. You slowly shut down these giant mono-crops as time permits, and eventually fix that soil so that area can be used for sustainable farming as well. That's called a hostile takeover. Corporations like Monsanto know what that's like.

You would need a lot more land and a lot more farms to make up for the loss in efficiency that these giant mono-crop and livestock farms can produce. But once you take the profit out of the equation, I honestly don't see food prices going up. Also, with the increase in the number of farms, we would have more food security. There would, of course, be some farming industries in which this wouldn't be possible – at least not for a long time. Farms in California that grow almond trees, for example, couldn't be so easily grown in the numbers that the world demands using these smaller farms. The same likely goes for cereals, grapes, coffee...the list could go on. We can only do what we can do – as in create as many environmental protection laws as are feasible.

With cheap, clean, and renewable energy, we could also have giant greenhouses that can grow food anywhere. Remember when I was talking about deserts that can power small cities just from mirrors and the sun? Imagine districts in the desert that decide to build skyscrapers that grow food using hydroponics and this energy. We would need to genetically modify many plants to grow in these conditions; but as long as the nutrients aren't affected, then that's not a problem. Right now, they genetically modify our fruits and vegetables to look good, and they sacrifice nutrients in order to do that – that's a problem. We could then export fruits, grains and vegetables to boost the income of these districts and create jobs. Or, we could plant fast growing trees anywhere in America and use that bio-fuel to power these buildings, even when it's freezing outside.

You could even pump the smoke from the burning of those trees into these buildings to promote plant growth. Plants love lots of carbon dioxide, and they would filter some of the greenhouse gases out of the smoke before being trapped and turned into synthetic fuel. This would have a triple benefit of having a carbon-neutral energy source (from burning trees), that enhances the growth of plants, and that you could create synthetic fuel from. This would also eliminate the dangers associated with growing food outside, in regards to pests, droughts and natural disasters. Not to mention use less land and water.

This income could make some districts a lot of money. The same can be said for producing energy in districts that have an abundance of the renewable kind. I said that food and energy don't belong in capitalism, but that doesn't mean that the people can't still make money off of them, just not individuals and corporations. These are necessary resources that belong to the people. Once a district has produced the quota of food or energy that they've been tasked with producing, then they should be free to make money off of anything extra. States and districts with more farmland are going to have to produce food for districts with huge populations and no land, like New York.

We would also be revitalizing all of these dying farm communities in America with an influx of 18-year-old kids coming in every year to buy stuff, and party (we'd have to change the drinking age to 18, which is what it should be). They do a year of growing food, and then get whatever skills training or education they want, within reason. The more clever kids would figure out new and better ways to farm the food, with incentives in place for doing so.

They would come out of that year knowing exactly what's working and what's not. Since there would be direct democracy (remember, kids, none of this happens unless we take control of the government), they would be able to directly input suggestions into how to fix what's wrong. In theory, it could become a well-oiled machine with the only incentive being that these 18-year-olds are going to become taxpaying citizens that subsidize this. They're naturally going to want it to run as smoothly as possible.

We'd still have kids going into military service and other government jobs – could you imagine 18-year-olds filling up the DMV kiosks, so instead of waiting an hour, you only wait 5 minutes? Or, answering phones so you don't have to wait all day on hold to talk to a government agent? You're investing in an educated populace that's going to pay taxes and repay whatever you've just invested in them, and then some. I'm not sure why North America hasn't adopted this strategy of free education – it's obviously working quite well for those European countries.

It's not sustainable to have so many people in a country who are afraid of school and of learning. The future is going to necessitate a populace that can learn new skills, because the robots are going to be taking ALL of those unskilled jobs in the very near future. We need to fix that with the next generation, or we're going to end up in a world like the film IDIOCRACY portrays. For those that have never seen it, it's about a future where the idiots have 10 kids, the educated/intelligent people have one or none, and the future is bright. No, hold on, I meant to say the future is terrifying and full of idiots. That sounds entertaining...for a movie...not real life. The problem is, that's already happening.

As far as resources go, I'm a very adamant believer that the natural resources of a country belong to the citizens of that country – not to corporations, districts, or states, but to all citizens of a country. There was a law passed 150 years ago called the Hardrock Mining and Reclamation Act. The aim was to promote the mining of precious minerals that America needed in order to grow. This act allows just about anyone, after buying a very cheap permit and jumping through a few hoops, to mine mineral resources in America. It costs under $2.50 an acre, that these corporations or individuals pay to the government, to mine an area. That $2.50 has not changed with inflation.

Over the years, a few Democrats have tried to pass legislation to change this act, and it's always hit the wet concrete of the congressional house floor to get stuck there. These companies are not giving anything back to the American people, only to politicians. In fact, they will sometimes leave a mine and not even pay for the cleanup. They pollute the rivers, lakes, groundwater, and soil of communities, leaving a pathetic EPA, that has no incentive or is buried in bureaucracy, to deal with it.

Not only that, but the law allows foreign corporations to come in and do the same thing. And they're not even mining the minerals that

America truly needs to become independent from the rest of the world, because China can do it for cheaper. The rare earth minerals it takes to build electrical components, especially those needed for renewable energy, mostly comes from China – as in 90% of it. North America already has the mineral deposits needed to become independent from China, we're simply not mining them.

No mining company is going to spend hundreds of millions of dollars to build a mine when they can't compete with China's prices. But this goes beyond profit – this is a national security, environmental, and world peace issue. We need to take the profit out of this equation. The government needs to build these mines, create a ton of jobs, and supply the materials necessary to become a country dominated by renewable energy. This investment will eventually be paid off.

I'll say this a few times in this book – the free world needs to break off all dependence from dangerous dictatorships like China and Russia. The slightly increased cost to make this happen will be well worth it in the long run. Plus, we'll be taking the profit out of these industries and hopefully keep them competitive. We can't allow these dictatorships to have this power over us, or world peace will never be possible. We need to own and invest into harvesting our own resources to make this happen.

Norway used to be a country steeped in debt. All of a sudden, they're one of the wealthiest countries in the world, despite being too socialist for my liking. It all comes down to one reason; resources, specifically oil. It's also because of very high taxes, which is mostly due to their overly generous welfare system – we don't need to go that far left and pay those same high taxes, we will create more balance than that. What's important here is that the country does not allow corporations to make profits off of oil – they use all of those profits for a pension fund. They also paid off all of their publicly owned debts with this industry. I have no doubt in my mind that America could do the same. Why are giant corporations making trillions off of the resources that should belong to the country? On top of that, they barely even pay taxes on those profits because of tax laws and write-offs. We can change that.

I'm going to keep repeating this – if the government is in control of anything, then there needs to be incentives for people to do a good job...or else it becomes what the current government is. So, if the people did own and mine their own resources, you'd still have to have forms of capitalism in there to incentivize the middle management. The middle managers are where all efficiency stems from. If they have no incentive to do a better and more efficient job, then the front-line workers under them won't care either. This, in a nutshell, is the number one problem with our current government employees.

Middle managers are the ones that crack the whip and figure out better ways to get the job done. As long as they don't have to go through miles of red tape to make changes, and they have the incentive to do a better job, then they become more efficient. When they do a better job, they should be rewarded accordingly. That's how you create an efficiently run social program. It's not through the useless people at the top, who usually have no idea what the hands-on, day to day activities consist of. I would even go a step further and say that each worker should be given production bonuses. Anything that the government runs needs financial incentives – it needs to be balanced with capitalism. So why not mine our own resources?

Nestle, the beverage company, goes across the world and buys ground and spring water from various countries. They pay very little for it, except to politicians (I'm guessing they do or else why would they be allowed to do this?), and they suck areas dry of their drinking water. How are they allowed to do that? Oh, right, politicians. Oil, gas, coal, natural resources, precious minerals, and water – how do these things not belong to the people of a country? A corporation should never be allowed to own or make profits off of resources. That needs to stop immediately upon taking control of the government. We'll talk about the logistics of making this happen at the end.

Another thing that needs to stop immediately is the poisoning of poor people. How is it possible that a box of Mac & Cheese is cheaper than an apple? How is it possible that a person can poison themselves for a lifetime, become obese with junk food, and the only ones to pay for it are other taxpayers? The corporation that has put this garbage out makes a fortune and gets away with zero repercussions. I'm not saying that we make junk food illegal, but it should be taxed like any other drug or substance that's bad for us – to try and limit our intake. Unhealthy food should be a treat; it shouldn't be the most affordable staple of a diet.

I'm not going to lie, I have an addiction to sugar. However, I have a high metabolism and an A blood type – my ancestors evolved to eat carbohydrates. For 50% of the population that has O blood type, and evolved to be hunter/gatherers, they can't metabolize carbohydrates properly. Not only that, but the gatherer also has a thrifty metabolism to store all extra calories for times of famine.

Want a little hint as to why there are so many obese people in America? They're the gatherers (25% of the population) whose bodies treat carbs like a drug, the most addictive drug they could ever do. They need to be helped, and so do I. We're like Gold Member from Austin Powers – we need the scabs taken away from us, or we'll eat them. If candy, which is my scab, were more expensive, then I would likely do less of it...or else end up on the street sucking you know what for sour dinosaurs. At least the candy would help with the bad aftertaste in my mouth.

We need to make healthy food cheaper and junk food more expensive. It really is as simple as that. We need to take the profit out of food production because capitalism in this industry has poisoned us and poisoned the planet. We also need to take control of the resources in our countries in order to become independent from China. Also, resources don't belong to individuals to become millionaires off of. If you want to make millions, then you should have some sort of special skill, or creativity, or an incredible work ethic. It should not occur because you're pillaging the earth for precious materials that belong to the people. I realize that this chapter was almost all socialism. Don't worry, it'll all balance out in the end.

Chapter 5
Money and Taxes

Just about everyone realizes that money is worthless unless we all agree that we will use it to exchange goods and services with each other. Most people can also agree that taxes suck. Especially when they're going to an inefficient system that just flushes it down the toilet – they have no incentive. Actually, that's a lie. They have a great deal of incentive, and their incentives are completely based on spending as much as possible so that they can get more in their next budget. It makes me nauseous remembering my time in the military, with the ambivalence and wastefulness. Have I mentioned that my life is ruled by efficiency? The government is the furthest thing from efficient, which nearly gave me cancer working for them.

Taxes definitely suck, but everyone has to pay them. You shouldn't be allowed on the street, or sidewalk, or get running water supplied by the government if you're not taking part in society. If you have a low paying job and don't make enough to pay taxes, but you're registered and taking part in society, then no problem. Want training to get a higher paying job? We're there for you. If you want to hide from the government and not contribute in any way, well, that's what this chapter is all about. Buckle in, folks, because it's a wild one...as wild as taxes can get, that is.

The American dollar used to be backed by gold. During the Vietnam War, President Nixon scrapped that logical idea in order to print more money to carry on the good fight. The American military-industrial complex was born, and Jesus brought forth an assault rifle and praised him. Ever since then, taxes for the wealthy have been steadily decreasing, which has forced the Federal Reserve to print money like it's 1999, and the world's about to end. It was done in order to increase the American military, pay defense contractors, and put Band-Aids on a faulty system.

The Federal Reserve is what they call a centralized bank. It was created in the early 1900s by the richest men in America, who decided they should control how much money was available. It was done in order to stem inflation and dictate interest rates for loans. They are technically supposed to be the big bank that controls all of the smaller banks in America. And Congress is supposed to control the FED, yet most of what they do is done without any government oversight or control. So, the question really comes down to – who is controlling whom? I would say that the big banks control both the FED and Congress. I don't think that's much of a shocking conclusion.

The FED typically makes 100 billion dollars a year from investments that they're able to acquire, due to the interest they collect on the money they 'loan' to America. To be clear, America technically owes the FED trillions of dollars that's considered debt, and we pay interest on that debt. Apparently, the people of America own these investments, but since there have been very few audits ever done on this agency, I really wonder how honest the whole system is. It's a bit complicated, and I'm not sure many people really understand what the heck is going on (me being one of them). However, I think everyone can agree it's a bit fishy that a private agency, that was created by some of the richest men in the world, who also own the big banks, can collect interest and make money off of printing our money. Granted, they don't actually print it, the Treasury department does, but they decide how much money they can print.

It appears on the surface to be a tad corrupt, and I imagine under the surface it's completely criminal. That is purely speculation, as it's not such a simple matter to dig underneath the surface of the Federal Reserve. That's really the biggest problem surrounding the entire agency, in my opinion.

Regardless, the FED needs to go if we're going to fix America. But it would be a very slippery slope to walk on if the people could print their own money at will. We'll talk about the rules regarding that near the end of this book, after we've discussed all of the industries we need to invest in.

Just before the end of World War II, the American dollar was chosen as the world's reserve currency. That means that international transactions are done using the American dollar as the currency standard. It also means that banks stockpile a bunch of American money because it's seen as a safe currency. When the dollar was backed by gold, this all made sense. Now, these banks basically control America because they hold so much of our money. Money that's mostly created out of thin air in order to give loans that probably shouldn't be given. People default on these loans in mass numbers, the tax payers bailout the banks, and the cycle continues. This is never going to stop as long as politicians and the FED are controlled by banks.

The GDP (gross domestic product) was an arbitrary metric that somebody made up in order to determine how rich a country is, and therefore how much money they can borrow. In America, each person alive grows the GDP. It doesn't matter if you're working or not, you grow the GDP. The government then 'borrows' money from banks, social security pensions, other countries, and from the Federal Reserve, because they spend more than they actually make, which is called the deficit.

Drunk Uncle Sam has a hold of grandma's credit card and doesn't really care about racking up the foreign owned debt, because he doesn't have to pay it back, and he's drunk. Grandma doesn't seem to care either because she loves her sweet baby boy, even though he has plenty of issues that need to be addressed. Plus, she's going to die soon anyway and won't have to pay it back either. Grandma makes decent money, so it's a platinum card with a near limitless amount of credit.

The problem is that it won't be grandma's credit card soon; it's drunk uncle's niece's and nephew's, who aren't even old enough to have a credit card. They don't seem to care either because they're too busy making TikTok videos. Or, perhaps they just don't see any way out of it, if they have ever thought about it. Don't worry, young ones, keep making your TikTok videos – your job will be very simple in changing this.

The only president in my lifetime to have ever balanced the deficit is Bill Clinton. That seems very odd since the entire Republican platform is to lower government spending in order to decrease the deficit. Yet, every republican president in the last 50 years has increased the deficit more than the democratic ones (besides Obama, who was handed a depression and war that he didn't start). Clinton's policies to balance that budget also contributed greatly to the recession involving the mortgage crisis in 2008. I'm not convinced either team really knows what winning means. If the purpose of the game is to drive your country into the ground, then they are definitely winning.

The GDP bases how rich a country is by analyzing all sorts of things like import/export ratio, average salary, tax income, population, and, most importantly, government spending. What's not included in GDP is the work a mother puts in to stay at home and raise children. Now, I'm no financial expert, but the idea that the wealth of a country is dictated more by putting money into a military institution, that does nothing for the economic future of that country, or into a prison and welfare system (that also don't contribute to future prosperity or happiness), than by mothers, who are raising the future workers and leaders of that country, seems a bit flawed.

Not to mention, the higher a country's GDP, the more they are supposed to contribute to things like the United Nations. But if a country is going into debt in order to have a high GDP, then why should they be contributing more? How is that actual wealth? If you own 10 beautiful cars, but they're all on a credit card, and you're using another credit card to make the interest payments, then are you actually a rich person? GDP is a ridiculous metric and needs to be either thrown out or redefined.

To keep increasing America's GDP, to allow for more borrowing, the brilliant government has created a military that spends more than the next 7 biggest militaries combined. They put bases in countries around the world and call these people their allies, because they're there to protect them from the countries that are looking to invade. It's a bit like an Italian mob movie: they go to a bakery, tell the baker he's in danger, if you know what I mean (that was done in an Italian accent), and if they don't give up the dough for protection, then something really bad might happen to them. Capisce?

So, these countries give money to America for this protection, which only partially covers the cost, and America is able to have a global military presence. To me, that sounds a lot like what the empires of old used to do, except America does it under the pretense of national security instead of world domination. Apparently, the bad guys can come take away your democracy at any moment – how that could happen, I'm not exactly sure. I never cared much for history, because I'm all about the future, but I know enough to know that all empires fall. America cannot continue this growing deficit in order to maintain their empire. And why would the American people want to?

What reason does the average American person have to want to put their taxes into an industry that does nothing for their economic future? It's a good question, and I don't know the answer. I suppose safety would be the reason given. If the majority of Americans feel safer now than they did 20 years ago, then I'll dunk my head in a toilet. Really, it would only be to try and get the money back that we've just flushed down the toilet with the military.

What about the prison system and social assistance? They're not actually investing into making Americans contributing members of society. They're making certain individuals wealthy within the private prison system. And they're masking deep-rooted problems that they're afraid to tackle with the social assistance programs, mainly, welfare. It's still government spending, and therefore increases the GDP, so might as well just keep doing that as long as we can keep borrowing money. There's no reason for politicians to stick their necks out and actually tackle difficult problems.

Can you imagine the uproar that a politician would have to face by saying that people need to start working because they're going to lose their welfare? That welfare needs to become a finite privilege, and you MUST become a contributing member of society, or you'll be cut off? That people on welfare can't have children? I think the majority would actually agree. But the far left, the loudest of all groups in America, would start calling these people Hitler, as loud as they possibly could, and that politician would be doomed.

To state the obvious, America can't keep this up, as no empire in history has ever been able to. Nothing stays good, nothing stays bad, and all empires fall – it's the facts of life. If given the choice, I honestly believe that the majority of Americans don't want to be an empire – they know it doesn't benefit them as individuals. They're not given that choice. Americans spend an incredible amount of their taxes on their military, prison system, and social assistance while their country crumbles. And China slowly begins to take over as the economic superpower. The rich get richer with a system of empirical rule, and the average taxpayer pays for it. The rich simply want to get as much as they can while the gettin's good. It won't really matter if America crumbles in 50 years, because they'll be able to buy their own islands to retire on.

The stock market is another place that only benefits the rich and hurts the average American. In the last 40 years, the wealth of the stock market, along with the wealthiest individuals, has increased substantially more than what stagnated wages should indicate, while cost of living skyrockets. That's an imbalance and therefore a recipe for disaster.

The stock market is gambling for the wealthy and really does nothing for the American economy in the long term – it only makes the wealthy wealthier. If you wanted to increase economic output, then you would get rid of the stock market and make the wealthy invest in tangible things: like real estate development, new restaurants, innovative new technologies, and entertainment. In a sense, that's what the stock market is supposed to do. Problem is, it's manipulated by those with the most money and power. They're there to screw over the little guy who thinks he's going to come in and make a killing in the stock market, not realizing that it's rigged.

The very first thing we should do upon seizing control of the government is, at least, enforce the rules that are there to make the stock market somewhat fair. Since these rules are enforced by the government that is paid by these rich people, I think you can imagine how well that's working out. I will admit that I don't yet know enough about this industry to comment on the rules, or what the rules should be. I do know that this system is creating a growing wealth inequality that can't be maintained and needs to be addressed.

The mighty Ronald Reagan cut the taxes for the wealthy by a great deal in the 1980s, with the promise that if they had more money to spend, then it would trickle down to the bottom feeders. Well, that didn't end up happening. What happened is the rich just kept it for themselves – hindsight is 20/20, I guess. Pretty much every major problem facing America today can be traced back to either Nixon or Reagan...but don't tell a Republican that because they'll likely shoot you.

I will say that the taxes did need to be lowered for the rich. Back then, the richest people paid 70% in taxes, which is criminal. Ronald dropped those taxes down to 50%, which by today's standards would scare away every rich person in America to another country. That wouldn't be good either. The point is that the wealthy need to be investing in tangible enterprises if you truly want a trickle-down effect from the rich to the poor in your economy – not into 'investments' that have minor tangible effects.

I've just listed some problems facing America's economy, and now, as is the structure of this book, I'm going to tell you what I think needs to be done to fix it. We'll start with taxes. Right now, in America, the rich do not pay their fair share. The corporate tax rate is 21%, which was recently reduced by Trump from 35%. Looking out for the average American, remember? Either way, if they actually paid 21%, then America could get a lot done with that money...I mean, not with the current system, but with direct democracy we could. Wealthy individuals pay more in taxes depending on their tax bracket, which differs in every state. You likely know all of this.

During the 2016 Republican presidential campaign, Senator Rand

Paul suggested America simplify its tax system, and everyone pay a flat 15% rate, with no tax write-offs. His argument was, the rich may be in a 40% or 50% tax bracket, but they literally pay almost zero. Why? Because of tax write-offs. The wealthy pay clever accountants that know how to 'invest' (i.e., hide) their money in areas where they don't have to pay taxes, such as stock buy backs. If you're a rich person and you've basically already bought all that you want, how much annual income do you actually need? Therefore, they don't actually claim a lot of income. Corporations and rich individuals do not pay their fair share because of tax write-offs.

You may say, 'but I get two or three thousand back a year because of tax write-offs, I don't want to lose that.' If you think it's better for the future of your country for you to be getting back $3000 a year, instead of that corporation paying hundreds of millions, then you are definitely the kid to take the one cookie. If the majority of America is full of the one cookie eaters, then I assure you, we're going to collapse. Then, you can loot stores and eat all the cookies you want...until they run out, and then you start eating people. Oh, I've got a new saying, 'eat one cookie now, then you are forced to eat one person later.' However, if you told a kid that he wouldn't have to eat that human for another 40 years, the kid would probably still eat that cookie. Oh crap, we might all be in big trouble.

Taxes can be so simple. An employee should never have to do taxes, only if you're a business owner. Then, the cost of doing business should be the only thing deducted from your income. The IRS already gets all of your information and does the taxes themselves, to make sure you're doing it right. Because you're a dumb cheater! Why even make you do them in the first place, then? Because of write-offs.

So, let's say the first $20,000 you make is non-taxable. This should also become the yearly minimum wage, which would equate to $10 an hour with a 2-week vacation. We won't need to raise the minimum wage to $15 an hour because these people will no longer be paying tax. This should also help offset costs to employers who will now be paying tax without write-offs, and not raise the minimum wage substantially to cripple them further. It does need to be raised slightly, though. Anyone on social assistance should get 60% of this yearly minimum wage – to encourage them to at least get a minimum wage job; because they're going to be working either way.

After that $20,000, everyone is taxed 25% (only on what you make after 20g) until your income reaches $100,000. Then, it goes up by 1% and it continues to go up by 1% for every $100,000 until it reaches 35%, at one million dollars. It caps off there. If you don't want the rich to run away to a country with lower taxes, then I suggest you make a hard cap at 35%. If there's a vote that increases your taxes, then everyone gets the same increase, in percentage, obviously not actual dollars.

You can't tax the hell out of the wealthy or they're going to leave. I feel like this is a healthy balance to them paying their fair share and keeping them in the country. I would also suggest that if a company wants to leave America, and go somewhere with cheaper taxes, then America boycotts that company. I don't mean going on Twitter and starting some hashtag. I'm talking about a federal boycott. You can do this while we still have spending power. If we wait 30 years when the collapse starts happening, then we'll have no more bargaining power to do anything like this. So, I suggest we get a move on with taking control of our government.

These taxes are done instantly, paycheck by paycheck, depending on what taxes your district and state are paying and the amount of your salary at the specific time of payment – not what the taxes are at the end of the year. If your taxes get raised by 1% in December, then you shouldn't be charged that 1% for everything you've made that year, only what you make after that vote takes place. It's constantly being updated because your tax account is joined with your voting account. Every employer will have easy access to your account, through your social insurance number, to deposit your taxes.

As far as people making less than $20,000 and not paying taxes – I say they shouldn't be allowed to vote on policies or laws that affect how much taxes you pay. Why would they? You can't just say you want a whole new highway and 4 new schools built in your district if you're not helping to pay the bill. That simply wouldn't work. If you want to have a say in what happens, then you have to be making enough to contribute.

I would say that a person should be able to opt in to pay taxes on their meager salaries, if voting means that much to them, but then how do you set how much a person has to make before they can vote? If they work for a week, make $500, pay their 25% in taxes on that, and then don't make any more money, should they be allowed to vote to increase your tax? I don't think so. I think the first $20,000 isn't taxed, and a person isn't actually allowed to vote on policies that increases income tax until they make another $5,000.

Technically, only that $5,000 is taxed at 25%, and if there's a vote that increases your taxes by 1%, then these people would only be paying an extra $50. That may not seem fair to the rich person who would be paying an extra $100,000. I say that the $50 means as much to that person's lifestyle, who is making $25,000, as the $100,000 is to someone making ten million.

Spouses who don't make anything? For every $25,000 in income earned, you get a vote. Therefore, if the income of the breadwinner is $50,000 or more, then both of those people should get a vote. Kids over 18 going to university and living at home? Again, for every $25,000 earned in family income, they get a vote.

An important point to make here involves how much voting power the poor should have. You can't take away all rights to vote on legislation – only those votes that increase taxes. If a vote comes along that would decrease taxes, and likely mostly negatively affect the poor, then they should be able to have a say. Therefore, they should still be allowed to vote on policies that would decrease taxes. We have to give the poor all of the help and resources necessary to get out of poverty, in order to create a truly healthy and robust economy. What's going on now, masking the symptoms with a constant influx of borrowed money, is costing more than it should without ever fixing the root of the problem. I think that's exactly what the banks and the federal reserve want.

I suggest a 25% income tax as a baseline to start out with. Depending on your district and state, that may go up immediately following the adoption of this system, or may go down. I would suggest 9% go to your district, 9% go to the state, and 7% go to federal taxes. A lot of that federal tax would simply be for the military, which should go down to ⅓ of what America spends now. Therefore, it's likely federal taxes would have to be more than this to pay for other programs, like social security. We could also figure out other ways to pay for social security, as I'll discuss soon, and keep federal taxes to a minimum.

Again, in order to create the most efficiently run government, you have to make it as small as possible. That means districts governing themselves, allocating their money where they need it, and not having to go through a bunch of red tape to get things done. State votes and taxes are there for the big laws that everyone wants to adopt in that state, and to help spread out the wealth to poorer districts. They're also there for health care, state police, disaster relief and to handle any disputes between districts.

At a Federal level, the votes and taxes are, again, for the major laws that everyone wants to adopt, and for major crises; which includes the obesity and homelessness crises. They are also for the military, foreign policy, and to settle disputes between states. I also suggest that the federal budget be used to spread wealth and resources between states. However, if a state is doing something wasteful and stupid, then they should be forced to change in order to get help.

I want you to think about this: when you put your money into a bank, or invest your money in something like the stock market, and it makes 5% interest, where do you think that 5% is coming from? It's either coming from somebody else losing money, the country going more into debt, or else from population growth. None of those options are acceptable in maintaining a sustainable society.

If you invest in bank stocks, then some of your return will be coming from interest made on loans. The government could, and should, create its own money lending program – that isn't run by a centralized bank which has its own self interests. If you have a job and are able to afford the loan payments, then the government should loan you money at a very reasonable 5% interest rate. If another institution can offer better rates, then people can go to them.

We make these loans exempt from bankruptcy and we should be able to get back the vast majority of this money – since we have direct access to a person's income. I don't see the point in having a fluctuating system with variable interest rates – it always ends up creating an imbalance. Let the market balance itself with a fixed and reasonable interest rate. There's no reason why a population can't be making the majority of money off of a government lending program. The only thing preventing that right now is the FED, which is controlled by the major banks, who control the politicians.

Technology is going to make industries more and more efficient, which is going to create a giant void in the job market. The government will need to be able to make money, that isn't just from tax income, in order to support a large portion of the population. We do that by taking over industries in which the top executives take the lion's share of wealth; such as food, energy, resource, and financial industries. The majority of jobs should still be available in these industries if they are run by the government, but the wealth that would normally be going to the few at the top will now be spread out among the people. The financial industry is going to collapse at some point, as it has already done numerous times. We need to figure out a better way to handle money and investments that isn't controlled by the insatiably greedy.

We invest our money for retirement and expect it to grow indefinitely, but that system simply can't go on forever. You can't just create money out of thin air and not expect the balance to be paid in some form – as in overpopulation or wealth inequality. So, how do we make sure people have money for retirement? We partially solve that through a sales tax. Just about everything an efficient government does should be taken care of through income tax. A sales tax would simply be to boost up a pension fund – consider it more as a retirement tax. Since collecting interest will no longer be a thing at some point in the future, we have to insulate ourselves before that crash happens. The longer we wait to make those changes, the harder that transition will be, and the bigger the wealth gap will become.

We simply need to create constant sources of guaranteed income, like through a sales tax, and not depend on interest, which depends on constant economic growth. You've already seen how fragile and dangerous this investment strategy is from the 2008 crash, when so many people lost their retirement funds. These economic crashes will never stop as long as we have this imbalanced system that depends on capitalism and growth. I suggest a sales tax go towards retirement because the wealthy will not be using this fund, so should not be disproportionately punished with an increase in income tax to pay for it.

Furthermore, there should be 5 - 10% added onto the production costs of food and energy to go into this fund as well. These are two industries that society will always be paying for, and are therefore always going to create money for old age retirement. Plus, we've taken the profit out of these industries so there should be some room to play with, especially when it comes to cheap, renewable energy production, and still keep costs what they are right now. Also, money from natural resources could go into this fund as well, like Norway has done. Unfortunately, these aren't industries that we can count on indefinitely, as resources like oil and minerals are finite commodities. The money made from natural resources should first and foremost be used to pay off foreign debt.

The social security pension is actually one area that the current government is doing an okay job at. However, there will come a time in the future where earning interest off of investments will no longer be a thing, as the population starts to decline. Plus, Americans currently pay a lot in taxes to go into this system, and it is eventually going to fail. I simply wrote this last part to get you thinking about interest on investments and retirement. Social security is something that shouldn't need to be immediately addressed.

That's a little taste of taxes; now, let's get to the really crazy idea of what to do with money. There's one major problem with the way cash is handled now, and that's criminal activity. Money laundering, counterfeiting, and people getting paid under the table – this is all made possible by the wonderful and previously necessary invention of cash. How often does the average, taxpaying citizen use cash anymore? I imagine it's getting less and less, especially among the younger generations. I personally never use cash, and I hate when I have to – usually at a Vietnamese restaurant that accepts cash only...mmm that's some tasty tax evasion pho.

I believe that in the not so distant future (10 to 20 years), we should be able to completely get rid of cash. I think most people realize this is coming and it scares them – I don't blame them. In the current system, with the control the government has over people and the banks over the government, I'm terrified too! The system I'm about to describe only works with direct democracy. If we don't have control of the government, then I don't suggest any of this to happen – keep cash and turn to a life of crime, the real American Dream.

Let's start with cryptocurrency. Unless you're big into this stuff, then you probably don't understand it all that well. What the creator of bitcoin devised is a digital system with a finite amount of money available (21 million bitcoins). The more people use them and want them, the more the value of these coins goes up. There is no influx of new coins; the value is naturally adjusted depending on supply and demand. Therefore, inflation takes care of itself, without a self-appointed governing body of rich families.

Another bonus of digital currency is the savings from the actual cost of printing money. America loses approximately 100 million dollars a year on just minting pennies and nickels. That means that the cost to make a penny or nickel far outweighs what those coins are actually worth. Not to mention, we're using valuable energy and metals in their construction. By our earlier calculation, just this savings alone would get almost 700 homeless off of the street.

Why is America still using a penny? Why is America still making nickels out of actual nickel, instead of steal? Like Canada does. Canada also got rid of the penny, saving many millions of dollars, and life went on. This is just one small example of government waste and ambivalence to debt. If Americans are so attached to the penny, then they can increase their taxes to pay for it – I have a feeling once that option is introduced, people will start singing a different tune. Many are blind to the repercussions of debt because the government doesn't seem to care either.

I am by no means suggesting the world adopt bitcoin as their main currency – that would be an absolute disaster. There are people out there who got in early and now own an incredible number of bitcoins. If the world suddenly adopted bitcoin, then these people would become instant trillionaires and richer than most countries. That wouldn't work. But, the idea behind digital currency and getting rid of centralized banks is a good one. However, it works best if the entire free world adopts it and gets rid of cash.

This is another super scary idea for those that believe in the deep state. The term 'deep state' is like the term 'God.' It has many different meanings, depending on who you talk to. If your definition of a deep state is incredibly rich people pulling strings from behind the curtain, then I don't think there can be much argument that it exists. What they exactly want is a bit unclear. Maybe they do want a global currency that they can control – that sounds about right, judging by what they did with the Federal Reserve.

With direct democracy, the deep state instantly dies. You can't create legislation by paying off a few dozen people, as direct democracy doesn't work that way. With a global digital currency, they would no longer be able to hide their money and not pay taxes. Therefore, that hidden money would become worthless with the adoption of this new system. If they can't prove where that money came from, and that they paid tax on it, then it can't be transferred over. I think that's a better punishment than putting them in prison. The system I'm suggesting is to control the rich, not give them more power. A global digital currency, controlled by the people through direct democracy, only hurts criminals and the rich, who don't pay taxes.

This is a radical plan, most likely 20 to 30 years away. Still, let's look at how it starts. Imagine a future where the majority of the free world has adopted direct democracy; or, at the very least, has freedom of the press and a highly functioning government that the people trust (hi, Switzerland, good work). The people of the free world decide that they want to make criminal activity, that involves money (not violence, that's impossible), a thing of the past. So, they create a digital currency and each country is allotted their share, depending on how much money that country has. It's hard to say what will be the global reserve currency at that point, but let's say it's the American dollar. We'll say that America is worth a trillion dollars. The United Kingdom is worth 500 billion, the same as France, etc.

A monetary system is developed that decides how much each country is worth, and that total is the number of credits that are put in this system. Then, each country is given its allotted amount of credits. The citizens of those countries then trade in whatever currency they're using for the global credit, which should be exactly what their currency is currently worth in the global market. If the free world decided to do this, then they would have to immediately freeze the value of all currencies while they decide how much each country is worth. Otherwise, there would be a great deal of currency manipulation and foul play. Likely, that's inevitable in some form and would have to be dealt with by whoever is globally elected to run this system.

The Global Treasury Department, let's call them the GTD, has doled out the necessary money to each country in the free world, and business resumes as usual, all in digital currency. This means no more opportunity for cash transactions. Everything you do can be traced, which is different than what bitcoin uses, and I'll describe why that's necessary.

Bitcoin was essentially created so that your money couldn't be traced by the government, and was instantly adopted by the criminal world as a way to do drug transactions, launder money, and not pay taxes. They did this using block-chain technology – meaning that every transaction goes through a bunch of different pathways until it's no longer traceable. That's the exact opposite reason I'm suggesting to adopt digital currency.

But, block-chain technology makes it almost impossible to hack. Then again, in the system I'm describing, it would be impossible to hack anyway; because the credits can't be taken out or put into the system. It can all be traced.

I'd like to add that hiding is not the intended purpose for using block-chain. Block-chain technology is the future of all transactions and record keeping, and how we counter cyber attacks. I'm not going to get into the technology, you can look it up if you're interested, just know that it can be used as the safest and most transparent way to do almost anything...unlike what Bitcoin uses it for. It would be the safest system to use for online voting. Back to the money.

I imagine that each country that's part of a future global economy, that doesn't use cash or traditional banks, would have a certain amount of credits to loan out to its businesses to help them grow, and in case of emergencies. I also foresee the united nations of a free world each paying between 0.1% and 1% in global tax, and that would purely be used to help countries that encounter catastrophes, or other hardships. It could also be used to spread the wealth between poor and rich countries.

The GTD would also have a set amount of credits to loan countries if they needed it. However, putting new credits into this system is a very tricky proposition, and opens the door for corruption. I think the GTD should be able to add credits only if a global catastrophe strikes, and countries simply don't have enough money to deal with it. Or, a dictatorship is toppled, and that country wants to join the free world. Then, like all other countries, they are given the number of credits that their country is worth in the global economy. Otherwise, it will simply not work.

The idea is to get everyone paying taxes. Let's be clear here, in my world of direct democracy, people have complete freedom over their lives as long as they're contributing to society, or until they're no longer able to take care of themselves. You want to buy some drugs? Go ahead, but the person selling it will be paying taxes on that income. You go for it, you little drug dealer entrepreneur. Whoever they get their product from better be paying taxes as well.

There would certainly be some things that should be illegal – child pornography coming first to mind. But prostitution between consenting adults? Why not? Tax it! How many billions of dollars are being lost to the black market right now for activities that we'll never be able to stop humans from doing? For every person that never touches a drug, there's another that over-indulges to the point of collapse – it's all part of the pattern and balance of life that we're never going to change. Let's at least make some money off of these bad behaviors to help pay for these individuals to get back on their feet, when and if they fall. A lot of people do drugs or partake in prostitution and are healthy, contributing members to society. I'm just not sure those naughty heathens are going to heaven!

This next bit is my favorite part of this chapter and I feel like it's a movie idea. I already have too many ideas rattling around in my head, and too many screenplays already written that need to get made. Therefore, I don't want to write this one, so it's free for the taking. TAX HUNTERS. Any individual, who goes through a background check and becomes bonded, can become a tax hunter. They'll likely be accountants or IRS agents that have lost their jobs from not having any more taxes to do.

They should have access to people's information like any other government agency. They can see who's paying taxes, how much, what they own, and their transaction histories in their bank accounts. Essentially, they are trying to catch people who are not paying taxes or not paying enough. Any cash transaction over $1000 should also have to be reported to this agency. Of course, this job would be geared towards the big cheaters, because tax hunters would get paid on a commission basis. I really don't feel that anyone deserves to go to prison for a non-violent crime (more on that in the prison chapter) unless they keep doing the same crime over and over.

So, let's say someone is selling cocaine and they're pretty big time; they own a house and have a bunch of high-end toys sitting in their driveway. Yet, they have no income or a very small income, like, say, from a part-time job. Where are they getting all of these toys from? Can they prove how they got that money? The job of the tax hunter is to prove that these people have made money and not paid tax on it. They then get 20% (maybe 50%) of all assets that that person has – the other 80% is sold and goes back to the people. If you refuse to cooperate with a tax hunter, as in not answer their questions, then they get an automatic warrant to search whatever they want. You don't put tax evaders in jail; you hit them where it really hurts, their wallets. You take everything they own and they get to start from scratch – what an exciting challenge for them!

I'm not suggesting you put these people and their families on the street. What I'm suggesting is you take everything that they've bought with money that didn't get claimed as income...and times that by 10. If it's everything, well then, they shouldn't have tried to cheat their country. They can have a modest home supplied to them, and survivable income until they're trained in something that can get them employed. That is if they don't already have any skills. Then, they have to start taking care of themselves; except this time around they'll be paying taxes. If they refuse to take part in society, well, I'll get to that in the prison chapter.

There are a whole bunch of fun little details I've thought about with the tax hunters: like tracking everywhere they go and who they're looking into, so that if they're 'silenced,' then law enforcement knows where to look. They need to record everything they do – including video recording all interactions with suspects. They also have to have all of their assets and income inspected with a fine-toothed comb every year, so as to prevent being bribed by the people they're looking into. Their lives would have to become an open book, and this job would likely only be for brave and honest folk, who want to catch bad guys cheating the system.

You may say, 'but the IRS already does this job.' Do they? Do they do a good job? What do you think their incentives are? Are they getting a portion of the assets that they seize? They are not. They have zero incentive besides just doing enough to not draw attention to themselves. Like just about everyone in government, their mission is to keep their head down, do as little as possible, and get to that sweet release called retirement.

As far as personal debt goes – in every revolution in history, when the divide between rich and poor becomes very large (like it is now), the poor take over and the debt is forgotten. The banks have made enough off of Americans in the last 50 years. Let them take what they have and run. In the monetary system of the future, with a global digital currency, there would be no more need for traditional banks. The 'banks' will simply become wealthy individuals who lend out money, which would naturally become a competitive space for the lowest interest rates to those that deserve it. There would be no reason for an 'independently' operated centralized bank to dictate interest rates. Saying that, not paying off your debt is illegal. So, instead of breaking the law, let's give people loans to pay off their high interest debt and make money off of that. Let's make high interest-rate credit cards no longer a thing.

Now, let's talk about global trade. There are countries not in the free world that are some of the biggest trading partners that America depends on. Why does America depend on them? Because of selling exports to them and because of resources. Rest easy, by the time a monetary system like this will be ready to be adopted, we'll be off the black tar and snorting that pure white hydrogen. Maybe we'll even be using fusion by then. Also, as previously discussed, we need to be mining our own resources and become completely self-reliant. Since the giant corporations that export most of what we sell to these dictatorships are barely paying taxes anyway, I doubt much will be missed in that regard.

Therefore, I suggest that the free world completely shut off all economic trade with countries that do not have a legitimate freedom of the press. Sorry, Russia, you're going to have to fix your system if you want to play with the good guys. Saudi Arabia? Give me a break. They've got a lot of hurt coming to them when the world gets off oil. China? Yeah, we might have to pay a little more for products, but world peace is worth it. Plus, by then, mainland China will be the new Taiwan, and cheap labor will have moved onto the next developing country...which they'll probably already own. If we don't act quickly, then China will likely own most of the undeveloped world and be taking all of their resources...with zero environmental protections. They're already well on their way to owning much of Africa. We need to stop giving more money and power to dangerous dictatorships, immediately.

We also need to stop trading with any country that isn't protecting its environment – that should be the only incentive Asia needs to fix its hot mess. Of course, America would have to set the standard before being able to enact such a thing. And our standard now is not something any country should follow. By the end of this book, you'll see what that standard should be.

I'll repeat this because I think it's very important, the free world must not deal in any way with countries that do not have freedom of the press. We cannot have world peace while these people are in power. Right now, China is Hitler's Germany and they are waging World War III, except it's through the economy. The amount of power they are going to wield will be no different than if they were actually occupying a country. The same goes for losing our freedoms and human rights. Removing them from global trade is the only way to win World War III, except there would be no bullets or bombs. If they did attack us physically, then please try and tell me that the dictatorships of the world, united, come anywhere close to the might of a united free world. We have all of the power; even with an American military that is cut by 70%, the free world would still decimate anyone that tried to attack us. The universe wants humanity to have freedom in order to evolve. This is a new age war, and we're trying to create world peace...peacefully.

So, how do we get from now to then without a total financial collapse? Firstly, we need to take control of the government – we have already established that. Secondly, we need to cut military spending by at least half, likely more, and put that towards fixing America's infrastructure. Where do the military jobs go? I'll get to that in the military section. Thirdly, we need to get all Americans contributing. All of those criminals selling drugs or their bodies (I don't think either is criminal) need to start paying taxes. I say we end the war on drugs, and whatever other silly laws that we can't stop people from following, and we create a war on tax evasion. We start a war on poverty, which could also be seen as a war on uselessness or laziness. Everyone needs to contribute if we're going to fix America. Or whatever country you're in, since this applies everywhere. We also need to start making money off of industries that belong to the people, in order to spread out the wealth. Here are a couple more Articles for our new Constitution:

Article VI: The biggest divide between the poorest and the richest can never exceed 10% in taxation. I think that this law is so important in order to keep rich people in America, and you want them here to pay taxes. I also suggest keeping the corporate tax rate low, around

30%, with no write-offs. No write-offs being the most important part of any tax laws we enact.

Article VII: Individuals that are not contributing taxes shall not vote on laws or policies that increase taxation. The income at which a person starts paying taxes will be dictated by law, through the people, and shall never neglect more than 90% of the population of that voting bloc. Every individual of age shall have the right to vote on all appointees elected by the populace, as well as laws and policies that don't increase taxation. This means that the bar that people start getting taxed at, say it starts at $25,000, can be changed, depending on the rising or lowering of wages and whatnot. But you must always include at least 90% of the population. This is to prevent the very slight possibility that many people stop making money, they're all under the taxation bar that was originally set, and the few who have money are then able to dictate all laws surrounding taxation. Bragging rights will come to those districts and states that get above 99% in people with taxable incomes. The other districts and states better pay attention to what those governments are doing...and do that!

What I'm suggesting in this chapter may seem like a huge infringement on your privacy and freedom. I would have to disagree. This system should increase your freedom, as long as we have direct democracy and as long as you're paying your taxes. If we have an efficient government, and everyone pays, including the rich, then everyone's taxes should theoretically go down – while also bettering the lives of everyone in America.

Plus, imagine those accountants becoming tax hunters: Ben Affleck, starring in, THE ACCOUNTANT part 2 – the Trumps thought they were untouchable until an autistic hit-man got a whiff of their tax evasion. Now they have to evade justice...tax hunter justice. It's all yours, don't mess it up.

Chapter 6
Education and Jobs

It's not a coincidence that the most successful countries on this planet have the highest populations of educated and skilled workers. They've invested in their future by helping (maybe forcing?) their citizens to become contributing members of society. America, on the other hand, has some of the highest education costs on the planet. It's also not a coincidence that America is 11th among developed countries with a population that has a post-secondary education. That used to be okay...in the 1950s.

Now, the uneducated are losing their jobs in unskilled areas like factories, assembly lines, and mines. Did they love these jobs? I highly doubt it. So why are they so upset about it? They're upset because they're afraid of their ability to feed themselves and their families. That should never be a concern in a developed country like America. The hate for immigrants that are taking these low-paying and soul-killing jobs all stems from this fear for survival. This is how I see a conversation going between a poor, rural American in a dying town, and an immigrant worker that is willing to work for less.

Rural American: YOU TOOK OUR JOBS!

Immigrant: But you American, you have chance to get better job.

Rural American: I'LL KILL YOU!

Then, the American shoots the immigrant. Unfortunately, it's not a very informative exchange about the realities of American life. Does that poor, rural American have all sorts of opportunities to better his life? Of course he does, it's still America. But he's obviously not taking it. Why? Because learning scares him...and it costs a fortune. Traditional education scars many children from a young age. Perhaps they're not able to keep up with the other students, and it frustrates them, which leads to acting out. This, in turn, leads to the downward spiral that that child will face in the coming years of struggling through basic education. You think they're eager to go back to that?

Or, maybe they had the ability to learn, they just didn't want to learn the useless garbage that traditional schooling forces down their throat. So, they skipped school and got high. Now, they're working in the kitchen of a restaurant, which actually takes some impressive organizational skills. Or, maybe school was too easy for them, they weren't challenged, and they became disruptive. Let's be honest, these people will never be afraid of learning, they were just bored.

America faces an incredible challenge over the next 20 years when it comes to their unskilled workforce. What do you do with them? What does a person do after losing their unfulfilling job in their factory? Or the mine, fishing, logging, or fossil fuel industry shuts down in their town, and they go on employment insurance, and then possibly welfare? What then? How do you get them off the free sauce? The government has programs to get them retrained in another career – good job, government, you should have been doing that in the first place. And those people have to jump through a hundred hoops just to get the ball rolling.

What about when the government doesn't force retraining on an individual? They will sometimes take the easy way out and less money to do nothing on welfare, if we allow them. Feed a wild animal continually, and it'll no longer want to hunt or forage for food. Humans are, at our core, just a more evolved animal. Well, some people are. When the option of doing nothing becomes available, many humans will unfortunately take it.

'That cookie was delicious, Government, thank you.' And then an hour later they say, 'where's my other cookie?' I'm sorry, weren't you listening? You get one cookie now and you have to wait to eat humans for another few decades. Sheesh, no wonder you can't get a job!

This chapter is about education, but more importantly it's about social programs. If we allow people to sit around and collect welfare, then how can we expect them to do more? Especially when they already have a fear of learning. We can bring back a lot of industry jobs when we start making our own products and mining our own resources. We're going to take profit out of the equation to remain competitive, and become fully independent. But that's still likely never going to bring those jobs back to past numbers. That's because robots are going to have most of those jobs in the very near future. Not only the brainless, repetitive jobs like assembly lines, but most transportation jobs will be gone as well – as computers become better at driving than humans. Don't think that will happen? Then you're probably one of the terrible drivers that doesn't realize how terrible most people are at driving.

Of course, the corporations of the future will still have to employ humans to sit and watch a robot work...in case the robot starts plotting with other robots to form a union. They'll have to employ some humans to take the load off of the government. It'll eat into their profits a bit, but that's the law – or should be. But who wants those brainless, unfulfilling jobs? Apparently, tons of Americans.

How do you FORCE people to learn new skills? This will be discussed more in the prison section, but we'll touch on it here. It all comes back to incentives. Perhaps some people will be motivated to want to better their lives without any external pressure – they just need the opportunity provided to them. What's the percentage of these people? Why the hell are you asking me? How can we possibly know that until we take that path? I hope it's a high percentage, though.

Perhaps others need a bit of coercion, like say, the threat of being cut off from assistance. I don't care who you are or what your disability is, I bet there's something you could do besides sitting at home watching daytime television, eating junk food, or doing drugs...unless you're in a coma or severely mentally handicapped.

In Taiwan, the government trains blind people to do massage, so almost all of the massage therapists are blind. I am by no means saying that this is what we should do with blind people. There are all sorts of programs and training for different jobs that blind people can do, even a software programmer. But what company is going to take a chance on hiring a blind programmer? The ones who want to save money because the government pays half the employees' wages, for those with a disability, until those employees become proficient at their job.

But the company then fires that employee in order to get another new trainee that they get at half the cost, right? There has to be reasonable cause to fire an employee. They have to be able to prove that the employee is not doing an adequate job, and that they've had plenty of warnings and opportunities to improve. Let's get rid of unions and give every employee the same rights that union workers have – minus the rule that forces the useless employee to get promoted before the much better candidate, simply because of seniority. That's a major failing of the union model and should never be implemented.

Democratic candidates, like Bernie Sanders, have been pushing hard for free education, and the young people like it. They should. It's worked wonders in other countries around Europe. The Republicans say that it'll cost too much money, and if you calculated education costs using the current model, then it certainly would be too much. However, those nonprofit schools are irresponsible with surplus income and are also quite inefficient. Not to mention, Republicans are obviously not taking into account the amount of money we already spend on an unskilled and uneducated population, that either ends up in prison or on welfare. Plus, education is an investment into your future – there's no reason why this money can't be printed. As I said, we'll talk about the rules regarding this, and how to pay it back, at the end.

Let's play math for a second with an efficiently run, nonprofit school. There are 200 students in a class. A professor teaches 3 classes a semester with 3 assistants. A professor makes $80,000 a year and the assistants all make $40,000, which equals $200,000. You divide their salaries by 600 students and that equals $333 per student to take a class. Add in the expenses to run and maintain the school, as well as any materials the students may need, and turn it into an even $500 per class per student (that last bit was pure estimation, and I think it might be too high). You multiply that by 5 classes and it's $2500 a semester. That's $5000 a year and $20,000 total for a 4-year program.

If the parents make enough money, then they should be forced to help the student survive (like they do in Switzerland). If the parents don't make enough money, then the student is given $100 a month for clothes and entertainment. Free housing and free food, if done efficiently, could cost as little as $500 a month. Over an 8-month school year ($4800) times 4 years ($19,200), you're looking at a cool $40,000. A person now has, let's say, an engineering degree. What other 4-year college programs would you take besides engineering, nursing, or marketing and business? Okay, there are definitely others, relax. We are going to need a lot of engineers to fix our world, though, so get on it now, kids.

This engineer makes $60,000 a year for the next 5 years until they pass their apprenticeship period. With the first $20,000 non-taxable, and at a 25% tax rate, they would pay $10,000 a year in taxes. The investment you just put into them is paid off in 4 years. Not to mention, many lectures could be run online, with no textbooks (online materials only) and many more students listening in for a fraction of the cost. Also, add in the fact that you've just gotten a year of very cheap labor from these kids with the mandatory year of government service, and it's a steal of a deal. That

$40,000 is what we already pay to put a person in prison for ONE year! A person that was likely never given an opportunity towards a proper education. If people want to pay to go to an expensive private school, then they can be given a baseline amount, that everyone else is given, and take a loan out to pay for the rest.

However, most college degrees are useless, let's be honest. You have to at least get a master's or doctorate to be able to use most degrees, and that path should only be available to the hardest working and capable students. A year, or less, trade school certificate would be much cheaper and more useful for the vast majority of kids. I'm not saying to get rid of the 4-year degree program in things like history or philosophy, etc., but I do think that after a person completes such a degree, the best candidates should be able to become a teacher's assistant right out of school. Perhaps, they make a modest $30,000 a year, which should give them some breathing room, but still motivate them to figure out what they want to do with their lives. Then, you have a lot more one on one help for those kids that struggle with school. Also, I don't think I need to mention that teachers need to be paid more. This is one of the most important jobs on the planet and we should be attracting the most capable individuals for this job.

That brings us to the problem we would encounter with this system pertaining to people not finding a job after they've been educated or trained in a skill. They should be given 2 months to find a job. After that, they become employed through government assistance and put in a position that likely won't be all that pleasant. They should make $12,000 a year (60% of the minimum wage), and this should encourage them to find a real job – hopefully in the industry they were educated or trained to work in. If they want training in something else, then they can take a low interest loan out for that...after they've worked for the government for at least one year. What we can't do is create cushy government jobs, that pay well and aren't necessary, for these people to sit in limbo for a lifetime.

I have a degree in psychology. I knew it was useless, besides it being interesting, while I was taking it. The military paid for me to finish it, and that's the only reason I did finish it. I originally did my first two years with the ambition of being a doctor. After 2 years of pre-med, at 19 years old, I finally thought about what it would be like to actually work as a doctor, and I got the hell out of there. The truth of the matter is, most 19-year-olds have no idea what they want to do. Even when they think they know, it changes once they actually start doing it.

Let's take a minute to talk about my favorite subject – me. When I was 20 years old, I took a commercial scuba diving course because I wanted a life of adventure. I knew I would only do the job for a couple of years, but it only cost $2000 to take (20 years later, it's now 4 times that amount and yet the wages have stayed exactly the same). I made $50,000 a year as a 20-year-old, working 4 days a week – not bad for a single guy after a 25-day course. I also didn't pay any taxes because I was a sub-contractor with a million write-offs – good for me, not for society. I then wanted to work on boats in order to learn navigation (as my ultimate goal was to sail around the world doing diving and sailing charters). I did a few courses, which took about 3 or 4 weeks, cost two or three grand, and got a job on tug boats. Again, I made about $50,000 a year...it could have been more if I chose to work more, which I didn't.

I got sick of the ocean and decided to join the Air Force to become a pilot. I spent the next 5 years of my life doing absolutely nothing. I made, again, about $50,000 a year, because I never got fully trained – long story, read my other book if you want to know more. Just kidding; stay away from that smut.

I got out of the military, went traveling, and then went back to school for electrical engineering, because I wanted to build a generator I had been thinking about. I did that for one semester, hated it, and decided to give writing a shot – I haven't looked back since. I finally found something I could stick with – I was 33 years old. But starting a career in writing is very difficult; especially screenwriting, which is what I focused on. I still had to pay the bills.

After some years of more $50,000 a year jobs, I reconnected with an old friend who had a job driving concrete trucks. With all of the overtime, it paid him almost $130,000 a year. I got my license and obtained a job doing that. I was taking home around $7500 a month, after doing a truck driving course that took 2 weeks and cost $2800. The point of the story is that college is not for everyone, and skilled trades are the future for the majority of people.

Also, don't be afraid to learn new skills – it keeps your mind sharp and keeps you employable. No matter what, I could always go back to one of those jobs and get hired, tomorrow. Until the robots start scuba diving, anyway. I guess they technically wouldn't need the scuba...crap, that job is almost obsolete too! Guess I better learn a new skill, since I can't write worth a damn. That's pretend humility. That's it for my minute of fame, back to the task at hand.

Some kids show an early aptitude for learning, others are more, let's say, hands-on. Some are purely creative. This 'one size fits all' school system destroys their ambition for learning. Let's be clear, the talent to do well in traditional school simply comes down to having a good memory. The education system, when I was in it, was all about memorizing and regurgitating – absolutely useless. Even though it suited me very well, I still saw the futility in it and was always incredibly bored. From what I can tell, this is slowly changing. Memory is not intelligence. There are all sorts of different types of intelligence and we need to harness what each kid is talented in – to make them enjoy school! But to not test them and give everyone a pass or fail? That's ridiculous!

In Germany, they start separating fast learners from slow learners early on. The accelerated kids are destined for jobs like engineer, pilot, doctor etc. The less scholastic kids have to pick a trade before they're even close to graduating, and they start learning that trade before they're done high school. That's a pretty efficient system. Why make a kid who's pretty much destined to be a janitor take high-level English courses? It doesn't make a lot of sense and turns the kid against education in the future.

You've basically learned everything you need to function in society, in terms of math and English, by the time you're past the 8th grade. I'm not suggesting that we do what Germany does, because it takes a lot of the freedom and choice away that America is based on, but some of these policies could certainly be adopted in some form. We will always be able to guide kids towards the jobs of the future that are going to be in demand.

I also think there should be a path available to those that show an aptitude for and love of learning. They can be lifelong students that are paid a modest salary to learn whatever subjects they want, provided they continually meet the stringent requirements. Every few years, they should have the opportunity to work on a study that can improve society, improve our understanding of life and the universe, or work on an invention of their choice. Of course, what they invent would belong to the people of America, with a small percentage patent going to these individuals. There's no question in my mind that a person with very broad areas of knowledge is best suited for innovation. They can see pathways that others who are immersed only in that industry can't see, by combining multiple strategies from many different backgrounds.

Something else I'd like to see is global engineers. We take the brightest minds and teach them every engineering and problem-solving strategy available, allow them to work in the required fields for a period of time, and give them the tools needed to fix the problems facing the planet. I think this is an exciting possibility for American innovation. But those are the workers of the future, who probably aren't going to be the biggest concern, since they can see where the jobs of the future are headed. What about the workers of today who refuse to adapt?

My mom is a dental hygienist. She sits in a chair all day, uses the same hand to scrape disgusting teeth, and the repetitive motion of the last

25 years in that job has left her body a mess. She's already had one surgery to help repair the damage and then went back to work 6 months later, still in pain. She could probably afford to get retrained in another vocation, but she's almost 60 years old. She sees the light at the end of the tunnel with retirement – just hang in there another handful of years, is the idea.

The fact that she was ever able to go that long in a job that requires the same repetitive motions is a failure on the government's behalf. I believe that a person should be given the opportunity for retraining after every 10-15 years of doing the same job. Furthermore, this retraining should be forced on people with jobs that require repetitive motion. Either that or the employee has to prove that they're doing the necessary stretches and exercises to prevent long-term damage – if they're really that afraid of doing something new. That's because this healthcare cost is going to be paid for by the taxpayer. It would be so much more cost-effective to just train them in something else every 10 or 15 years – something that uses a completely different set of muscles.

Construction workers who have been bending over their whole lives basically crawl home at 60 years old because their bodies are destroyed. Truck drivers who sit all day have done the same to their bodies. Let's be clear, an unhealthy job can consist of activities where you sit all day, as well as stand, because sitting for long periods is extremely harmful. There are, of course, ways to mitigate this damage. You could stand up every 30 minutes and walk around, or even stretch, but most people aren't doing these things. Most people get home from an 8-hour day, and all they want to do is relax. They don't want to stretch or work their core muscles to protect their backs. I don't blame them.

That's why it should be a law that an 8-hour workday consists of an hour-long, paid break to do physical exercise of some sort – whether it be a walk, a stretch, or a full-on cross-fit murder session. The employer should help foot the bill to help prevent damage done to an employee's body. Studies have shown that people actually do the same amount of work, and in some cases more, when they're given a substantial break in the day to get in some physical exercise. Police, firefighters, and military personnel already get this paid time to exercise, through our tax dollars – so why not give it to everyone?

If your job is already labor-intensive, then use that hour to stretch or strengthen the muscles that aren't being used. Maybe just meditate and work on your emotional and spiritual well-being, which are just as important as physical (the triangle of health). We'll discuss this further in the health care chapter.

In regards to the kids doing a year of government service, they should get a couple weeks of training near the end of their final school year, so that they can seamlessly start working in whatever placement that they're put in. The person who trains them in that job should be the kid from the year before that's doing that job now.

We should also focus more on life skills in grade school. Learning all of this useless information that a kid forgets the second the exam is over is a waste of time and money. Let's teach them how to be good at actual life. Let's focus on critical thinking so that they can't be fooled by con-men running for political office. Let's get them to question everything they're told and to think for themselves, but also teach them how to find the truth. To base their opinions on fact, instead of what someone in authority or the media has told them, or what their parents have tried to brainwash into them from childhood. Let's teach them what happiness actually means – we do this through courses on positive psychology, which are based on actual studies of what makes people happy. I'll give you a hint, it's not money. Let's focus on creating highly functioning adults, instead of a simple memorize and regurgitate educational system.

America is losing most of the jobs that made it great in the first place. America used to be the main exporter in the world, and factory jobs created a great middle class – 'edumacation was for 'dem fancy pants!' Today, a factory job puts you near the bottom of the rung in socioeconomic status. Unless you somehow have a union factory job, in which case you now have the golden handcuffs shackled on your wrists. So, you're likely filling your void, created from an unsatisfying job, with all sorts of unhealthy behaviors.

Every developed country has taken its turn in becoming a large exporter and lifting its citizens out of poverty through factory work. Right now, that's China. And China will face the same problem in the coming decades – a large, unskilled workforce that has lost the majority of their jobs. The question comes back, how do we fix this going forward? It's not going to be pretty, I'll tell you that much.

The right-wing part of me wants to froth at the mouth at liberals for allowing the welfare system to exist the way it does. Yet, what have conservatives done to change it when they've had the power? This game gets kind of boring when neither team ever actually does anything. We've created a generation of people that have learned to do nothing and get by on it. How do you force them to now have to do something? To learn new and complicated skills when they're afraid of school? It won't be easy, and it's going to take some tough love.

What about the others that have had jobs and they're full of fear and anger because they've lost those jobs to robots or immigrants? They're in areas that have no other opportunities. This, along with the aging and unhealthy population, is the most difficult problem to solve. A highly functioning society, with a surplus budget, simply cannot afford to have more than a couple percent of its population living as leeches. There are certainly going to be opportunities to help them, but some of these people are going to refuse it – 'force me to learn? I don't think so, bud! This here is a free country!' We're going to need to create hard rules that force these people to start contributing. That'll come in the prison chapter.

Old industries are dying. Taxi drivers fight Uber drivers because they're taking their jobs. Do they realize that all of these jobs will become obsolete when cars drive themselves? Unless you're 60, then there's very little chance that you'll be able to retire as a taxi driver. Why are they focusing their energy into a dead end? Because they're afraid to learn. In this quickly changing technological world, you adapt or die. There are going to be new industries creating jobs. That has been, and will always be true. Look for the opportunities and jump on the timing. Timing, you know, is everything.

For unskilled workers who are likely only good for unskilled labor jobs, we're going to create a lot of work in the resource sector. More importantly, the green industry is going to boom. Installing solar panels on roofs could certainly create a lot of jobs for the next 10 to 20 years. The government should be giving interest-free loans to people to have renewable energy sources put on their homes – their loan payment would simply be what they normally pay in an electricity bill. They shouldn't need tax incentives to do this. As I've said, if we want to truly create a country running off of renewable energy, then homes are mostly going to need to power themselves.

There will be millions of new jobs created in the green sector. Yet, the Trump administration has reinvested in the coal industry, saying they're going to bring back jobs in these dying towns. They lost those jobs because they became automated. Therefore, the coal industry didn't all of a sudden produce a ton of jobs because of a lift on environmental protection. What kind of promise was this? Does he have stocks in coal or something? Or was it simply that he kept hearing this same complaint during his campaign and jumped on it?

Since he was unable to tell the truth about what the future looks like, he used talking points like this to unite a scared population that wanted their jobs back. Yet, study after study has shown that the boom in job growth is in green energy, so why go back to dead industries? And his followers salivate over that promise, which went nowhere. Why? Because they're afraid of learning new skills. 'Bring back 'dat easy life, The Donald, if anyone can do it, you can – you're a genius!' They just don't want to have to be uncomfortable and learn again. Please, God, anything but that! They're going to need some tough love, I'm telling you!

On a brighter note, I honestly believe that when people are given a second chance with school, after they've hit rock bottom, they take it more seriously the next time around. Most education really isn't that hard, it's just a matter of putting in the work. A lot of capable kids didn't want to put in the work when they first went through. I'm hopeful that when someone loses their brainless job to a machine and really starts to assess their options (that don't involve a lifetime of handouts), they'll put the work in to get retrained. They better, or we're all in for a rough future.

Tech jobs, as in fixing machines, anything in software, or the other millions of jobs in technology, will be available to those that aren't afraid to learn. Simple. For the artistic minds, I have ideas on how to allow for livable wages (chapter on that, of course). America needs to truly invest in their brightest minds to lead the way in innovation – that's where new industries come from.

There will be tons of jobs available in the preventive health care industry (government jobs), jobs training others in their new vocations (more government jobs), and even more jobs associated with fixing our environment, mining our own resources, and creating clean energy. The money to do this is all coming from decreased military spending. Also, from the majority actually contributing to taxes, including the wealthy. The money will also come from a healthier population that isn't spending all of their taxes on healthcare (I hope you're as excited for that section as I am). Lastly, it'll come from the government creating money to actually invest into its future, instead of putting Band-Aids on problems – we'll no longer be hindered by a FED that's controlled by the insatiably greedy. The rules regarding creating money are very important and we'll get to that.

For those that simply refuse to learn, there will always be sidewalks that need sweeping, recycling that needs sorting, and schools that need cleaning. In my functioning society, you better have a good reason for staying at home and not doing anything. This is because education and skills training will be made available to everyone. As will all necessary programs to get you healthy, either physically or mentally. So, what do you want to do? Become a plumber? An electrical technician? A Madame at a brothel? Fluffer for pornography? Just remember to keep the sour dinosaurs handy for the aftertaste.

Chapter 7
Healthcare and the Elderly

Healthcare is a hot topic in America, as it should be – there is a large percentage of unhealthy people in this population (large having a double meaning). As we talked about in the food section, cheap junk food and sugary drinks are creating an obesity epidemic. This is only going to keep getting worse until forceful action is taken to create healthy lifestyles.

A diabetes epidemic is coming, and it's going to largely affect the poor, who mostly eat processed, cheap food. This diet also contributes a great deal to heart disease and cancer – 80% of all diseases are preventable through lifestyle. Not only is poor diet and a sedentary lifestyle destroying health in America, but a growing elderly population also creates near-insurmountable obstacles to overcome.

There are a few options to consider: We continue the way we are, keep going more into massive debt as sick people, who aren't working, consume a great deal of resources to stay alive. That's a pretty lazy approach, and if the average American's fear of change is that severe, then this is where we're headed. Remember, the politicians aren't going to make the difficult choices that need to be made.

We could say, 'you've created this yourself, you, um, you large person, and if you can't pay for it, then you get what you deserve.' That's incredibly right-wing, and I'm not on that side for this one. Another option is to create Medicare for all and simply increase taxes by a fair margin to take care of these people. That's a very far left-wing response, and I'm not on board with that one either. I like the middle option – we create healthcare for all, but in order to be eligible you have to live a lifestyle that promotes sustainable health.

I've already discussed how I think it should be a law that employers are forced to give a paid hour every day for physical activity. I've also discussed how junk food should become a treat instead of a staple, by making it more expensive than healthy, whole foods.

So, how do we actually enforce a healthy lifestyle? That's a really dangerous proposition when it comes to freedom of action. If a person is severely overweight, and they're still working, then why does the government have any business in their life? They don't. But if that person wants 'free' healthcare, then they have to meet the requirements to get that. It's still their choice, but they're going to be contributing taxes to this system whether they're using it or not. If they want to continue to be obese and live a lazy life, addicted to unhealthy foods, then they should have to pay extra for their own healthcare. If they can't? Sorry, you've had fair warning about what the rules of social healthcare require.

What happens when they need healthcare – they're dying, they didn't follow the rules and can't pay themselves? To counter this, I'm sure there will be bleeding heart organizations out there that spring up to help these poor souls. What about the church, that likely has trillions stashed away in their private Vatican banks? Their whole platform is to help the needy, isn't it? I personally say, let these people go. They'll know better in their next lives. I also think a lot of people would rather eat crap, be lazy, and die at 60, then go through all of that extra work. So, let them. People should always be given a choice, and if an early death is their choice, then why should you force them otherwise?

To say that these poverty-stricken individuals should have to dig themselves out of this hole would not be fair. That's why they should be given all of the tools necessary to make themselves healthy. There should be therapists available to get people out of their depression with a focus on meditation. I mean proper, focused meditation on their emotional injuries – not this nonsense about sitting there with no thoughts for an hour. Then again, exercise and a better diet will instantly boost depression levels.

That's why there should be personal trainers available to whoever wants one, as well as free gym passes. There are going to be a lot of empty buildings in the not so distant future, with the internet taking over commerce. So, we should turn those buildings into fitness centers. Or, personal trainers can come to people and show them how to workout in their homes. Dietitians and meal planners should be available to whoever needs one. Physical therapists should be available to those that have pain in their bodies and simply aren't able to exercise. Physical therapy, especially when you get a good therapist, is by far the most beneficial when compared to massage therapy, acupuncture, or pharmaceuticals. The sad part is that the people that need it most can't afford it. However, you've got to do the work yourself with physical therapy, and that's why it can actually heal you long term. It's not a temporary mask of pain like those other options – just about everyone simply wants to take a pill to solve their problems.

The idea of giving people pills to mask the problems going on in their bodies is western medicine's way of dealing with sickness. It's a recipe for disaster. Eastern medicine has an approach where if you get sick, then your doctor is to blame for not keeping you healthy. I like that approach. We never get to just take a pill, without any sort of work or sacrifice, and expect there to be no consequences down the road – that's not how life works. For every good thing that happens to you, there has to be work and sacrifice to get there. If it sounds too good to be true, like taking a pill to solve all of your problems, then it is.

This masking of symptoms is creating havoc on the healthcare system, and that can't be a model of health for the future. If you're wealthy enough to afford your own health insurance, then, by all means, do whatever you want. As I've said numerous times, unless you need help from the government, then they have no business dictating how you live your lives. Wanting others to pay for your unhealthy behaviors would be negatively affecting others' lives on this planet.

Now, if junk food is taxed and people continue to eat too much of it, then those taxes should help offset the costs of healthcare – the same way with drugs. Right now, people smoke and drink too much, and it gives them health problems later in life. However, those things are taxed and should be taxed more heavily. Someone who smokes a pack a day should pay roughly $5 a pack in taxes, which, if you do the math, works out to about $55,000 over a 30-year period of smoking. That may not sound like a lot to pay for the treatment of lung cancer, but that's applying the inefficient and for-profit model that exists now. Not to mention that in the not so distant future, we'll be able to grow organs in a lab and do transplants for relatively cheap.

I also believe that we're going to get much better at cancer treatment – there are already all sorts of treatments that involve diet and holistic approaches that use your own immune system to fight disease. Your body, when healthy, has everything it needs to cure almost anything. That doesn't simply mean physical health, but emotional and spiritual health as well. This is obviously not the method used by western medicine, but it should be in the future.

One of my goals in life, besides hydrogen and water in Africa, is to build a self-sustaining community that focuses on research in healing disease. If I do nothing else but this, then I would probably consider that a pretty successful life. I honestly believe that there is enough research already out there that shows how to defeat cancer through a plant-based diet, meditation/therapy, exercise, and stress management – that's what this property would focus on...among many other unconventional treatments.

Stem cell treatment, which has been blocked by the religious sector, is also another very likely avenue for future healthcare that could drastically cut costs. Another way to increase efficiency is to get rid of the general practitioner. They have become a redundant and unnecessary middleman.

All doctors should specialize, even if it's in something like elderly care. And we can cut down the amount of school that focuses on areas they don't need to know. A computer program, like WebMD, can direct people to the appropriate professional that can treat their ailment. A pharmacist can prescribe drugs. A general practitioner does nothing but send you to someone who can actually help you – what a waste of time and money in this technological age. I've never in my life had a family doctor. I have to go to a walk-in clinic to get the simplest of prescriptions that a pharmacist could easily give. It drives me crazy!

I've talked to numerous GPs and they tell me the main thing people come in to see them for is depression – they just want someone to talk to...and, of course, get those sweet pills to mask the pain. Why are they not going to a professional therapist? Because it's not covered, even though it should be. Depression is a major illness that shouldn't be masked with pills. There are treatments out there that don't involve pills, and people should be given access to them under socialized healthcare.

There's been surprisingly little innovation in the healthcare industry in America in the last 50 years, besides pharmaceuticals. That doesn't make a lot of sense, since it is indeed a capitalistic enterprise. Once you start thinking about how the industry makes money, it all comes together. They don't make money from a healthy population, and from treating someone quickly and efficiently that never has to come back again – that's not a very successful business model. They don't really want to heal sickness. On the surface, it appears that they do, and I'm not even sure that they do it purposefully or maliciously. They're just making money, and are blinded to what they're doing.

I'm sure doctors really do want to heal people and find better treatments to do so, but they're not the inventors. The doctors that have been inventors typically come up with groundbreaking innovations that change society – like the discovery of insulin and penicillin. So, why not fund the brightest doctors, who have shown an affinity and interest in developing innovative treatments? They need incentive, though, so they get the typical small percentage patent for whatever they come up with. I feel many of them would simply do it for the joy of knowing that they've saved lives – being a doctor typically attracts these types of people.

I believe that if America invested substantial money every year into designing NEW ways to cure disease, there would be quite a bit of innovation. I don't think innovation by the large corporations is focused on the curing of disease – they're more interested in designing quick fixes to mask symptoms that keep people coming back and paying for a lifetime.

Stem cell treatments need to be fully adopted. We've had enough of this nonsense of a fertilized egg being a human that you're killing. You're indirectly killing many millions of actual living humans, and keeping many more millions in pain, by not adopting these treatments. If you let religion keep legislation in the dark ages, then you're going to get passed by many other countries. Then the rich are going to go there for treatment – which they already are.

Mental illness is easily the most complicated subject to touch on, probably in this whole book. I'm not going to pretend I know what to do with these people – those that are too far gone to ever be a contributing part of society. They also cost a great deal to take care of for a lifetime in an institution. I know that these people, mainly the homeless, weren't this far gone when they were younger; otherwise, they would have been put in an institution. There's no question that doing too many hard drugs has fried their brains, and they're likely never recovering completely from that.

The right-wing part of me says that if a person will obviously never get better, then just send them on their way and wish them luck in their next life. The left-wing part says, okay, I'll pay another couple percent in taxes to keep these people alive and drugged up for life. I don't really know where else to go with this. It's always going to be a contentious issue because I don't believe there are cures for a lot of the mental illnesses out there. The rising homeless population mostly consists of mentally ill individuals, and there's no question that they need to be taken off the street – nobody should be allowed to live on the street.

If I had to make a stand right now, I would say let's really invest in new forms of treatment that focus on the root of the problem, like psychotherapy, hypnotherapy, and guided meditation. If a person refuses help, or is obviously never going to become functional in even the minimalist of ways, after something like 5 years of treatment, then I say put them out of their misery. I could also be pretty easily convinced to pay another couple percent in taxes to drug them up and keep them drooling in a padded room for life. It's a tough one.

Let's move on to the other major problem – the elderly. I'm not sure if you're aware, but there was this generation of humans and all they did was fornicate. They were called the Silent Generation – I guess they had quiet sex. They lived through the Great Depression and Second World War. Apparently, they were very determined, hardworking, and simple. They shouldn't be characterized by that, though, they should be called the Horniest Generation: #horniestgeneration.

I guess it's because birth control wasn't invented yet (besides thick condoms that no man was wearing, plus religious practices don't allow birth control), and pulling out isn't as fun (but if done properly, it's as effective as condoms in preventing pregnancy). There was the Great Depression, during which everyone was probably pretty bored with a lot of time on their hands (if you know what I mean), and there was significantly less child mortality than in the past. These reasons aren't nearly as fun as simply calling them the horniest generation. They had a ton of kids and gave rise to the baby boomers.

Many countries are now in a battle trying to figure out how to deal with this sick and aging population. If you want to know why immigrants are allowed in your country at all, this is the reason. Most couples these days have 1 or 2 kids, educated couples I should say. These are also the people who pay the most taxes. One or two kids isn't going to cut it when it comes to increasing tax income to pay for the elderly; hence, immigration. Which is funny since the baby boomers are typically the most unwelcoming to immigrants – you realize they're here to help pay for you, don't you?

Let's play math for a quick second again. Don't groan, children, math is fun! A person works for 50 years, they average $10,000 a year in taxes paid, that equals $500,000 put towards government spending. They then cost at least that, and likely much more, in the 20 to 30 years where they stop working and the healthcare system pays for them. Dammit, that wasn't a very fun math game. Granted, I wasn't counting the money that they made and put back into the economy, let's try and keep this simple. It's pretty clear that this is a recipe for financial ruin.

So, how do you fix that? Let's be clear; if an elderly person has saved up for their own retirement and can afford their own healthcare, then this does not apply to them. For those that have done no saving and require the government to look after them, then the same rules apply to them as everyone else that wants social Medicare. They have to eat right, exercise, and do activities to keep their minds healthy.

The retirement age is late 60s for most of the developed world. If there's a forced retirement age, that definitely has to go. As long as a person is willing and able to work, then they should be allowed to work. Let's say that a person has worked from 20 to 68 and now wants to retire through government assistance. They have no money saved, and the amount the government will give is likely just enough to live – no money for traveling or the big-time life that they always dreamed of, even given up their entire youth waiting for. That's the reality that many elderly people face – they've worked in a job they didn't like, counting down the days for retirement, to do what? Sit around and watch TV, take the dog for their daily walk, and live on an extremely tight budget, praying for the day that it can finally all end. That doesn't sound like much of a life.

Studies have shown that the happiest elderly individuals are those that spend their retirement giving back to the community. So how about this: you reach 68, or whatever age is decided, and you're allowed to retire with government assistance that is paid for through a sales tax – say $1500 a month. There would definitely need to be federal tax that's contributing to this as well, because a sales tax on its own would have to be very high to support this. And don't forget about the money from food, energy, loans and resources that we now own. These people should then be allowed to work in elderly care homes (or forced?) until they're no longer able to help, and have to go into one of these homes themselves.

They work 20 hours a week, with substantial vacation time, and their monthly income goes up to $2300, which would equal $10 an hour. They keep the residents company, play games with them, exercise with them, change their bedding, cook, feed them, clean, etc. They do everything except the demanding jobs, like carrying the residents from chair to bed, or security – I imagine taking the blue pills away from horny old men during herpes outbreaks isn't a peaceful process. Once a person goes into one of these homes to live, they then only receive spending money, say $200 a month. The rest of the money they were receiving from the pension fund now goes to their retirement home.

I also believe that assisted suicide should absolutely be offered. Right now! I can't figure out, for the life of me, how a society that makes assisted suicide against the law, also claims to be humane. How is it humane to force a person to live in pain, or severe dementia, or confinement to a bed? You ask most able-bodied people whether they would rather just be put to sleep than live like that, and almost every single one of them will always give the same answer. Nobody wants to be a burden.

There has to come a point where we let people decide when they've had enough with this life in this body. We should help them get there, painlessly. Of course, this opens the door to possible corruption with children performing 'assisted suicide' to parents who aren't ready, because they want that damn inheritance. I'm sure we can figure out rules around that. If you can't, then give me a couple weeks and I'll think of some. Right now, this isn't a priority in my life.

These assisted living homes can't be decrepit brothels of depression. We have to do our very best to make these places hospitable and fun. I believe that having the newly retired work there will create internal checks and balances to how these places function – since they'll likely be going to one of these places as well.

It's an unfortunate fact that kids in the west simply throw away their own parents, but that's the way it is. In Asia, they look after their parents because the government doesn't do it. Perhaps we make a law in America as well that forces children to look after, or pay for, their elderly parents. Of course, only if they have the income to do so. I would likely be on board with a vote like that. I wouldn't throw my mom into some decrepit home after all that she's sacrificed for me, even if I had to get a second job to pay for it. That's just me, and probably many of you as well. The major cost for the elderly is always going to come through healthcare.

Unfortunately, I foresee a future where healthcare is truly tailored to the rich, and the poor are given Band-Aid solutions that never solve the problems, for which the taxpayers will continually pay for these treatments...hmm maybe that's the present. We have to take profit out of the treatment for sickness and disease and make laws that focus on efficient ways to actually cure ailments, instead of masking them. This is going to take work and sacrifice by the individual, because nothing good comes without work and sacrifice. If a person doesn't want to put in the work and just wants a Band-Aid solution, then they better have the money to pay for it themselves.

The rich will have access to all new organs whenever they need one. In the distant future, they will likely be able to get whole new bodies, but I don't foresee them ever truly transplanting a person's personality – your memories do not make you who you are. Babies and toddlers react to the exact same experiences differently because of how we are innately wired in our souls, which is our connection to the collective conscious. Transporting memories into another brain doesn't create the same thoughts and will never create the same person, that's my prediction. We're getting way too metaphysical and into the future here, let's focus on the next 30 years and good old-fashioned science.

If a person has paid their taxes, and they've had some unhealthy behaviors, like eating too much junk food, smoking, drinking or whatever else that has been taxed because it's unhealthy, then they should be given one organ transplant – provided they've met the lifestyle requirements for socialized healthcare (which shouldn't be too hard to meet). Remember, these organ transplants will be fairly cost-effective in the future. I'm just not sure it's wise to give everyone unlimited transplants and raise life expectancy to 150 years. Are they going to require assistance for 70 years? Much longer than they worked and paid taxes? That simply wouldn't work. However, the wealthy are likely going to be able to get transplant after transplant, and as long as they keep their minds healthy, they'll probably live quite a long time. If they can afford to do that, then they should be allowed to.

There have to be some benefits to being rich, besides just buying nice things. Almost everyone aspires to be rich, and if they're all of a sudden limited to the same life as everyone else, then the motivation to work hard, to innovate, and to sacrifice for a better life becomes moot. It becomes too socialist; I personally don't want to see a society swing too far in this direction – where everyone is essentially a union worker, all equal no matter what, and devoid of all inspiration and work ethic. That is certainly not the American Dream.

I believe that healthcare should be a state's responsibility. Remember that 9% you're putting towards state taxes? This is what most of that would be going towards. It may not be enough, and this may have to be raised until a healthier population is created. However, I think that with a more efficient system, profit taken out of the equation, and the actual cure being implemented instead of Band-Aids (with a great deal of work and sacrifice put in by the individual to heal themselves), healthcare costs can be cut down dramatically. Healthcare, as it stands now, is the biggest expenditure of the American government – they spend twice as much as Canada per person on healthcare, yet it's not even socialized healthcare, like Canada has. How is that possible? It all comes down to profit.

Anything to do with healthcare should have profits taken away; including, the production of hospital devices, pharmaceuticals, and all treatment plans. You may say, 'then where does innovation come from?' It comes from the same strategy I've mentioned before – a small percentage patent for the production costs of anything an individual or corporation develops. If someone develops a better machine that does CAT scans, and many hospitals adopt it, then they should make money off of production costs. It can't be the sale, and therefore profit of these machines, because they're not for sale – they belong to the American people under a system of socialized healthcare. But you still need that incentive for innovation. What if private clinics come up with treatments that are only available to their rich clients? Those technologies have to be made available to the American people at cost, with the patent percentage going to the innovator.

The federal government will be in charge of spreading out wealth between states. Some states, Florida being the obvious example, have an older population. They're going to need more healthcare money than say, New York or California. Let me say this to Middle America, that has a strange hate-on going with the heavily populated coastal states – they're the ones that are going to keep America afloat in the troubling times ahead, so let's not go overboard on the liberal bashing. Let's make a song about getting along, 'we're all a little left, and we're all a little right, so let's ditch the teams, and we'll all join the fight.' What a fun song!

The federal government spreads the wealth around to those that need it most. If a state needs money and it's past a certain threshold, per capita, then they should be forced to raise their state taxes. Districts should still be in charge of keeping their constituents healthy, and enforcing health laws where applicable...as in someone living a very unhealthy lifestyle and taking part in social Medicare. This, of course, would require yearly checkups on weight, blood, urine, and physical fitness. You don't want to take part in this? Then pay your own health insurance. If you can't afford that and yet don't want to follow the health laws in order to get social Medicare, then you get sick and die alone. I told you before, and I'll tell you again, the future is going to demand some tough love for those that want to have their cake and inhale it too. Tons of cake.

Then again, maybe America is a lot more liberal and compassionate than I predict. If some states choose to give everyone Medicare without any sort of health requirements to meet, then they can pay the extra 5% or 10% in taxes. This will, of course, be a state decision, not federal. Maybe that's the way many votes would go. I doubt it. Those that are the least likely to put in the work to be healthy are those that are the least likely to be paying taxes. Therefore, they wouldn't be allowed to vote on such a policy; since it would increase how much taxes you pay. You've got to drag them along kicking and screaming; or, in this case, wheezing and stuffing their faces before we take the cake away. Come on, I didn't make one fat joke this entire chapter, give me this one!

Chapter 8
Prison Reform and Law Enforcement

America has the most people in prison than any other nation. We all know that's because of the drug war, and, more specifically, the war on minorities...African Americans and Latinos being the main target. I'm not going to sit here and pretend like the ghettos in America, where drug use has gone out of control, aren't major problems. I am going to say that perhaps this method of imprisonment, which has very little emphasis on actual rehabilitation, has made matters worse. The private prison system has become a for-profit industry, and just like the healthcare industry, they make the most money when you keep coming back.

All prisons have education and skills training available for inmates to prepare them to get back into the world. Unfortunately, many of these programs are very flawed. There are prisons that teach inmates how to be barbers, but in their state felons aren't allowed to be barbers. What's the sense of teaching an inmate how to do something that they won't be allowed to do in society? It's a mirage of helping, when in reality they just want that golden ticket to come back into their greedy little hands.

I'm going to share a little story with you that encapsulates the foundational flaws in America's prison system. I drove down the Mexican Baja all the way to Cabo San Lucas. I went there to live for cheap and do some writing. Upon arriving, I soon made friends with some Mexican guys that saw me walking on the street – they had the intention of selling me timeshare packages, I'm sure. Three of them became my good friends, and I learned all of their stories in detail.

They had all gone to America as very young children and grew up there. They had all gotten mixed up in the drug trade and gone to prison. Actually, one of them had skipped bail and escaped down to Mexico. You can thank him for saving all of those tax dollars. The other two did 5 years and 7 years in prison. The one who did 7 years had been transporting cocaine in the trunk of his car and had a tail light out. Cops pulled him over, first offense, and he got 7 years. After both of these guys served their time, they were instantly deported out of America and sent back to Mexico. Now, if someone can tell me what the heck the point is to spend hundreds of thousands of taxpayer dollars punishing a person, with the guise of rehabilitating them, just to kick them out after you've done so, I would love to hear it.

The guy who had done 7 years was actually a model citizen. He was a painter and didn't do anything illegal in Mexico. I guess Mexico should thank the American taxpayers. He had gotten his G.E.D. while in prison, and he truly was rehabilitated. Did it really need to take 7 years to do that? No goddamn way. He grew up in a poor area where the drug trade is what you did to make money. He was a really good guy and had all sorts of potential to help society.

The other one that did 5 years grew up in a black ghetto in America. He spoke like he was from the ghetto and they all made fun of him for it. When he was sent to Mexico, he didn't even know how to speak Spanish. If that's not the most absurd thing you've ever heard, then I don't know what is. The point of the story is, if you're going to spend money to rehabilitate 'criminals' by putting them in prison, then they should actually be turning them into taxpaying citizens of America. If you're just going to kick them out, after you've spent all of this money on them, then why not just kick them out before you've spent a dime? Because they have to be punished for what they did? Is that what the average American wants to spend their money on? Punishing people for selling drugs? Are you that vindictive and petty? If you are, then, by all means, raise your taxes and put your money into that. If you want to actually invest in these people, to stop them from being a black hole in society, then it's going to take some patience, tough love, and investment. The investment is already happening, in larger quantities than it should take, and it's not producing anything in return.

With the way the judicial system is set up now, people do non-violent crimes, such as theft, or drugs, or tax evasion, etc., and go to prison for a ridiculous amount of time. This has quite obviously become a profit-making industry off of our tax money...as well as keeping the GDP nice and high in order to keep that platinum credit card status. I've already mentioned that I don't think non-violent offenders should be put in prison. But there's a limit to that. If a person keeps trying to evade paying taxes or continues to sell illegal, hard drugs after already being caught, then there needs to be an escalation in punishment, no question.

I mentioned the legalization and selling of drugs by the

government, but that can only go so far. I can't imagine a person doing heroin, crack, or crystal meth and still being functional for very long. I don't think a country can legalize hard drugs like those. Natural drugs like marijuana, tobacco, alcohol, mushrooms, peyote, etc. should be sold by the government. I'll even add MDMA and a few other drugs that aren't overly addictive or harmful. That leaves cocaine – a highly addictive drug that also damages the body. But studies have shown that it's not more addictive than sugar, nicotine or caffeine. Caffeine is, in fact, in the same family as cocaine, with just a few different double bonds between atoms. It's a white powder that you can snort and get the same effects as cocaine. I personally think cocaine should be legal and sold by the government, within reason.

This is why: The war on cocaine is destroying countries south of the American border. This, in turn, creates hordes of immigrants trying to escape their war-torn, corrupt countries and come to America. This, in turn, makes Americans hate immigrants. Why do you think they want to leave their beautiful countries? Mexico is amazing and has so much potential. You think these people want to leave their homes? They have to because of the war on cocaine. So, I think cocaine should be legalized simply for that reason. Americans are going to do it no matter what, as they apparently really love it. I don't know why, I personally think it's a terrible drug. So, why not make money off of it and help those countries out in the process?

In the society that I envision, there should be no reason for a person to have to steal or deal illegal drugs to get by. If they want an easy life, like selling drugs and not paying taxes, then they have to learn that life in a functioning society doesn't work that way. The opportunities are there for them to get trained through social assistance. If they're truly unable to hold a regular job, then get them working in garbage dumps picking out the recycling on a commission basis. There are tons of jobs like this that we could give people. Nobody gets to stay home doing nothing unless they've got some sort of crippling disease.

Another stipulation of collecting social assistance should be random and frequent drug tests. In my society, a person has complete freedom to live how they choose...until they are no longer taking care of themselves and need government assistance. Once you reach that point, you give up your right to do any drugs or alcohol until you become a functioning part of society again.

So far, what I'm suggesting is very left-wing – besides the drug testing – but it isn't balanced. You simply can't have a functioning society with policies that allow people to be indefinite drains on resources. Let me rephrase that, you will have to increase your taxes to pay for these people to be indefinite drains; because going into more debt, to put towards policies with no chance of a return on investment, is no longer an option.

To create the most efficient system possible there has to be some kind of deadline for people to get their act together. Before I talk about this, I want to make it very clear that this is simply an idea, and not what I expect to happen...at least not for many generations – not until the world really starts collapsing. If we can prevent that collapse, then hopefully this idea will never be necessary. Talking about ideas, having healthy debates, and figuring out solutions is my goal here. Do not think that I expect all of my ideas to be implemented – this is simply about starting that discourse into solving problems, if we really had the power to do so. Okay, now get ready for some controversy.

My idea is a 3 strikes and you're out policy. I'm not talking about 3 strikes and we put you in prison for life, that's an inefficient use of taxes. If a person is never going to be rehabilitated, then just send them on their way and wish them luck in their next life. It's very harsh, but seriously, we've now given them every chance possible to get the help they need, and they have refused any attempt to better themselves.

At what point do you say, 'enough is enough?' Are you a person that is willing to raise your taxes by 1 or 2 percent to keep these people in prison for life? Then, by all means, vote for that. I have a feeling there are many left-wing states that will do this. I'm curious to see how long that lasts and if it can actually work in the long term. I hope they figure out humane and efficient ways to do it, I really do. However, I can't imagine why a person would want to spend life in prison over death.

Prolonged punishment should not be a goal we strive towards. It should be quick and efficient, with every opportunity for rehabilitation given. Punishment is a symptom of a sick population, or a sick individual; therefore, we must always be digging into the root of that problem. Our ultimate goal is the evolution of the human species and the human soul. The soul learns the important lessons upon reaching a dead end – death – the same way it learns if it's in prison for life. I personally don't see the difference, and there's no possible way I would ever spend life in prison.

Myself? I would vote for the death penalty. There are simply too many people on this planet and too many problems to tackle. We cannot be wasting that much time and resources on individuals who don't want to help themselves. Plus, I honestly believe it would take a minimal amount of executions before people got their act together.

This is how I see the 3-strike policy working: an instant strike is a violent crime, like armed robbery, aggravated assault, and sexual assault (not actual rape). Anything to do with illegal weapons should also be an immediate strike. Manslaughter or rape – an instant two strikes. Child molestation – instant 2 strikes...although, I would personally vote for euthanasia. You better start running, Vatican church. Murder in the first-degree beyond a shadow of a doubt – euthanasia.

You may say, 'but people are convicted of first-degree murder all of the time and are later found to be innocent. What if you kill one of these people?' When I say beyond a shadow of a doubt, I'm talking about people that have murdered in front of multiple witnesses. There really is no doubt about it and you don't even really need a trial to prove it. If there's the slightest possibility that they didn't do it, then wait 5 years and allow them to prove their innocence. We should also collect DNA samples and fingerprints when people register with the government, in order to help with crime fighting. But we don't want to do that right away...just getting everyone to register will be an uphill battle, and forcing them to get fingerprinted or swabbed would be a deal breaker. Either way, there are plenty of instances where the death penalty is obvious.

I remember there was a man on a bus that cut a teenager's head off, that was sitting in front of him. The bus driver stopped and everyone ran off the bus, screaming. The police arrived and this guy was walking around the bus carrying this head, muttering nonsense. They put this guy in a mental institution. He was obviously insane and we spent millions of dollars on trials, institutions and whatever other nonsense that went down the toilet. He had a mental illness. So what? Anyone who commits first-degree murder has a mental illness to some degree.

Why does mental illness excuse murder? I don't get it. There are too many people without mental illness to help right now, and spending exorbitant amounts of money and time on these people is not an efficient solution. Why are we spending billions of dollars on people who have committed crimes, instead of putting that money towards people who are living in poverty and not committing crimes? Does that make any sense to you?

If you say we should be spending our money on both, then you better be ready to raise your taxes. Some readers right now are truly horrified with my 3-strike proposal, but you'll always have the option to pay more taxes and keep these people drugged up and incarcerated for life. If your state doesn't vote along with what you like, then move to a state that does. I guarantee some will exist. I don't expect you to agree with me, or like my ideas, I only expect you to accept other people's opinions that differ from yours. The majority will decide what they want to do, not one man's opinion in a book. That's democracy.

In my world, the police should have just shot that lunatic and saved everyone a lot of money. Or else skipped the trial, gave him a couple days to make his peace, and sent him on his way. Those many millions of dollars, to look after this one insane individual, could have brought dozens of families out of poverty. Then, those families are paying taxes, instead of draining them, and putting money back into the economy through spending.

It's an exponential increase in the strength of your economy through these few million dollars that were spent on one crazy individual. And how often does the government waste millions of dollars on frivolous things? They spent many millions on a pointless investigation into Trump that was never going to accomplish anything with a cowardly Republican Senate in charge of impeachment. Those millions could have lifted hundreds of families out of poverty.

Capital punishment is just one difficult avenue that a society of the future will have to contemplate, with limiting resources and rising debt. How much are you willing to spend on people who have committed heinous crimes, and there is absolutely no doubt that they've done it? Personally, I want to spend no more than 10 dollars on someone. This would be to put them to sleep and then to kill them painlessly. Yeah, this got dark really quick. This is a morose chapter – some aspects of life are very dark. Deal with it.

Sticking your head in the sand isn't going to make the problems go away. There is no upward trajectory for a society without hard decisions and sacrifice – the sacrifice in this instance being the ability to silence your compassion for the greater good. Or else pay more in taxes.

In all honesty, we should be able to create a thriving society with many more opportunities for people to at least support themselves. Not to mention, the end of the war on drugs will have a major impact. So, the cost towards the prison system should decline rapidly. This might actually become a minor expense in the grand scheme of things, and a 3-strike rule may be a moot talking point. It might also become the biggest problem we face, with millions of people who simply refuse to contribute anything and continue to commit violent crimes. What do you personally want to do with these people? Direct democracy will give you the choice of where your taxes go and decisions like this are something you have to think about. Just please don't assume that I expect you to agree with me.

I only know one thing; we must be more balanced between masculine and feminine, right-wing and left-wing, than we are right now. A pure right-wing individual would say, "Why even give them free training and school? If they can't pick themselves out of the gutter, then just get rid of them." A pure left-wing person would say, "You can't kill people. That's insane! I will absolutely pay to keep them alive and in an institution for life." Both of those extremes lead to an unbalanced population. On the right-wing extreme, you're setting yourself up for a ruthless society, devoid of compassion or opportunity for those born into poverty. If it had always been that way, then you might be able to get away with it, as plenty of dictatorships do. But we've been too left-wing for too long and created a large population of poor who are used to getting handouts. So now, we've set ourselves up for a civil war with the poor, which turns into martial law, which turns into you losing most of your freedoms. This is where America is heading now without a drastic change in regards to equal opportunity and wealth inequality.

The left-wing extreme leads to an unsustainable practice of putting money into people who, let's be honest, simply don't deserve it. You go into extreme debt (unless you raise your taxes), the economy crashes, China owns you, and you lose your freedoms. The balance is to give people the opportunities by actually investing in them, not just the bare minimum, but a real investment of $100,000. If they still refuse to contribute to a functioning society, then you wish them better luck in their next life. In my opinion, that is the balance.

That $100,000 is 2.5 years in many prisons, which is how long they put people in prison for drug possession (simple drug possession, not even trafficking). You can hopefully create a functioning member of society in that same amount of time. If you can't? You still only spent a fraction of what you're paying now on these people, with little chance of them ever contributing. And you actually gave them a real opportunity to improve, not just the mirage. If they don't want to take it, then you've at least given them a choice. They'll know better in their next life. As I said, and will keep reminding you of, you don't have to agree with me on this. Democracy and the will of the majority is all that matters. But if you disagree with what I'm saying, then you better have another solution. Just saying that won't work but offering nothing in return, and refusing to pay more taxes for these people, is not acceptable.

If you're afraid that the majority will simply start executing people at whim, then I think you are not giving Americans enough credit. This 2-

party system and intuitive tribalism in America has created an incredible divide between people, who mostly have the same beliefs. A person who calls themself right-wing isn't just a heartless, capitalistic machine. I guarantee the majority of them won't want to simply execute poor people – they'll want to give them opportunities to contribute and better themselves, but they realize that can't go on forever. And a person who calls themself left-wing has right-wing beliefs as well. They likely won't want to pay for people to sit around and do nothing for a lifetime. We have to realize that we have a lot more in common than not. Getting rid of this idea that we belong to a political party is the first step in accomplishing that.

What about actual prison? To put a person away for any more than 5 years is an absolute waste of money. If that individual can't be rehabilitated in 5 years or less, then there's something seriously wrong with them and they're likely never going to improve. What I would really like to see happen is quick and efficient punishment. On their first strike, they commit a violent crime like armed robbery or assault. For that, they do a month in solitary confinement.

Putting prisoners with other prisoners has to stop. It becomes a school for them – they learn how to become better, lifelong criminals. In solitary, you give them enough room to be able to exercise. You give them an hour or two a day with a therapist. You also give them all of the reading and media available pertaining to self-help and self-improvement. They get a nice long adult time-out. When they get out, they start the process of education and training to get them back into society. That is if they don't already have a job to go back to. We also need rules to prevent employers from discrimination based on prison time – they shouldn't even be allowed to ask.

If they want no part of this society and want to kill themselves, then let them. Give them the tools to do so in their room. They can decide whether they really want to be here or not. With 8 billion people on this planet, we don't need individuals who don't want to be here and would rather just cause chaos and destruction. If you want to make the argument that letting people die lowers America's GDP, then I'll counter that it's pretty clear how stupid GDP is, if it thinks a person is contributing to the wealth of a society while being in prison or on welfare for life.

Some will say that solitary confinement is torture and makes people go insane. With the way it is now, I would probably agree. What I just suggested is far from that – they get an hour or two a day to talk to someone who actually wants to help them. Then, they go back into their room to think about what they just talked about. I believe it would have a much quicker effect on their ability for self-analysis and desire to improve. The money to transform prisons to accommodate this can be created by the government. The money we then save from not putting people in prison for lengthy periods will go towards paying off this public debt.

When it comes to the second strike, it's time that the punishment gets more serious. They do 6 months in solitary confinement, with the same allowances as before, but with a much more streamlined approach to where their problem really lies. Are they addicted to drugs and that's why they're committing these crimes? Then focus on drug treatment. Rage issues that lead to assault? Then focus on anger management and meditation training. These things will obviously be addressed in the first strike as well.

They will be very aware that this is their last chance at life. The third strike, you're out. I'm not talking about these death row sentences that cost millions of dollars. These people will have already had numerous opportunities to better themselves; how much are you willing to spend on them? If the answer is, 'whatever it takes to keep them alive,' then, by all means, vote for that. I'll gladly pay for whatever people decide to do.

If you're afraid of direct democracy because the majority might be on board with what I'm suggesting, or could vote for other policies you don't agree with, then you don't really want to live in a democracy. What you actually want is to live under a dictatorship in which the dictator only makes laws that you like. Good luck finding that. We need to remember what living in a functioning democracy means – it's a give and take in which you win some and you lose some. We don't have to like it, but we have to accept it.

If you're like many people, and feel like you know the right thing to do, but that person beside you is too stupid to be in charge of decisions like this, then you are part of a very common bias that I see everywhere – people seem to think everyone else is so much different, or less capable than them. That's simply not true. The majority of people are in the middle, the logical place, and they'll be the ones dictating laws. There are 30% on each side that are either too far left or too far right, but those 40% in the middle are who make the magic happen. Those 40% will often swing either right or left on different policies, but they'll almost always end up coming back to the middle – that's where we evolve the fastest.

Most politicians aren't going to touch the subject of capital punishment. This will come down to the people – where do you want your money to go? There are approximately 50,000 people in America serving life without parole. They will average, at minimum, a cost of one million dollars each. That equates to 50 billion dollars. What do you think that 50 billion dollars could do to get people out of poverty? This one isn't a difficult decision for me. Each state and district will do something different. If you don't like what your state or district is doing, then move somewhere else.

I've already talked about how I think tax evasion should work with tax hunters – turn capitalism onto crime-fighting, and you'll see something really get done. You take their assets and you don't put them in prison. This also allows a person to prove their innocence without a ton of long-term damage being done. You can't give a person years back of their life that they lost in prison (if later found innocent), but you can quite easily give them their assets back.

What if they do the same crime again? Or another non-violent crime and lose more of their assets? They now have two soft strikes. After three soft strikes, they get their first real strike and do their month long time-out. That process starts again for 2 strikes, and if it continues all the way to 3 strikes, then they're out. Personally, I don't think they need 9 opportunities – that's a bit extreme. Once they get their first 3 'passes' and get their first strike, then they should probably just start getting hard strikes after that...when it comes to the same offense.

If someone is selling illegal drugs, then it's a soft strike; because the only real crime they're committing is tax evasion. Therefore, they lose their assets instead of prison time. If they have no assets, then they work for free, with food and shelter being provided, until their debt is paid off. Why are we spending money to punish people? Isn't that a punishment for us? It doesn't make any sense – they should be the ones paying. I would, however, suggest that selling illegal drugs to anyone under 18 be considered a hard strike. Selling legal drugs to anyone under 18 should be considered a soft strike – you lose your assets. Let those young brains develop fully before they start getting destroyed.

Marijuana, as physically harmless as it may be, really affects the motivation and ambition part of the brain, which a teenager needs most – in order to put in the work to learn things that they have no interest in. I can't count the number of friends I had that smoked pot in high school and never wanted to do a thing because of it. Now, their opportunities are very limited because that all-important base is not there. This is the base that allows you to pursue the well-paying vocations, which good high school grades afford you. If you don't have the natural ability, then it really does just come down to putting in the work. Do you think China is full of geniuses? Or is it more likely that they just work harder at school?

Many will consider what I've just said to be a pretty drastic action towards crime and the prison system. My addiction to efficiency overrides the compassion in me, in this regard. There are simply too many poverty-stricken areas in America to be dilly-dallying about. An entire city,

Baltimore, essentially needs to go through this one month time-out and rehab. It's ludicrous to think that it was ever allowed to get that way. America has allowed the downward slide to continue for so long that the actions needed to correct that slide now need to be more drastic. That same principle carries over into all difficult aspects of life that we want to ignore, and will only get worse the longer we ignore them. We're too right wing when it comes to the environment and capitalism, and too left wing when it comes to social assistance and punishment. These are the exact opposite sides we should be on when it comes to long-term sustainability.

With all of that being said, I'm willing to raise or lower my taxes depending on whatever my fellow citizens vote on – that's the payment to live in a democracy. Some states will figure out some pretty clever ways to rehabilitate and punish efficiently, and I can't wait. Some will waste countless millions on dead ends – it's all part of the learning curve. As far as who controls the prison system, that should be the state, not the districts. Districts should be in charge of people until they get their first strike, and then they go to the state for their spanking.

Senators will be our elected officials in charge of the judicial system. I don't believe we need to create constitutional laws regarding this branch. I would like to see states be able to figure out their own systems of appointing judges and doling out punishment – that's how we'll evolve the fastest and find the best solutions. I also believe that judges should have a lot more freedom to work in the gray area of punishment. Not all people who commit the same crime deserve the same punishment – there needs to be more commonsense regarding this than just mandatory minimum sentences.

Imagine this scenario: a father kills a man that raped and murdered his 12-year-old daughter. Does that father deserve the death penalty or life in prison? I think most people would say no. He does need to be punished for seeking vigilante justice. But not to the same extent as a man who does a home invasion, robs and murders a family. Judges should be able to use commonsense to deal with the gray areas of life. Our justice system is too black and white...I don't mean that in a racial way.

Also, think about this: there will be many far left-wing people who will hoot and holler over the death penalty, but then be willing to fight to the death over abortion rights. How does it make any sense to allow the death of a human that hasn't started breathing yet, but deny the death penalty to someone who was given a chance at life, and used that chance to murder innocent people? On the other side, you'll have pro-life activists screaming how important all of God's creations are, and then want every criminal strung up in a noose. People are full of humorous contradictions.

That's all I'll say about prison reform. It's an area that is going to require lots of innovation and adaptability. If something isn't working, then quickly change it. This system is obviously not working in America, and yet the government does nothing to change it. They're useless. That uselessness all stems from the system itself and a focus on re-election (i.e. trying not to make any big splashes that could create controversy).

As far as law enforcement goes, I have quite a bit to say on that matter. There is one failing of law that I personally want to address, and that few will agree with me on – the idea that preventative crime measures are worthwhile. Sure, they may stop some crime, but at what cost? Being driven by efficiency, I am a strong believer that you don't bother someone until they've actually done something bad, like hurt someone, and then they get punished severely. Spending money on law enforcement to prevent 'crimes,' that are just as likely to not even occur, seems insane to me.

Take drinking and driving as an example. Most people agree that drinking lowers your effective decision making and reflex response. So, there's a war on drinking and driving. Does it prevent some people from drinking and driving, knowing that they could lose their license or pay a fine? Absolutely. But how much are we paying to enforce that? How many lives has this ruined for people who technically didn't affect anyone else? What if, instead, you say, "Look, you do what you want, you've technically not committed an actual crime yet, which involves actually affecting other life. But if you do, then you're REALLY going to pay for it. If you disobey a traffic law while over the limit, then you lose your license for a year. You want to drink and drive and you kill someone? You get 2 strikes for manslaughter." Although, some might say instant death penalty for that.

If you get in an accident and hurt someone but don't kill them? You lose your license for life, get a strike, and the other lovely aspects that go along with that. You want to scare people who shouldn't be drinking and driving? Will something be more effective than that? Who would want to take that chance? Punish them after they've actually done something, not because there's a possibility of something happening. Many terrible, sober drivers are allowed behind the wheel, but they're quite obviously more dangerous than some others who have had a couple of drinks.

You let people have freedom until they do something to lose it. You get in an accident? Instant drug and alcohol test, doesn't matter if you're showing signs of impairment – you've gotten in an accident and you've negatively affected someone else. If they're shown to be above legal limits, then they get punished severely.

Let's be honest, cars are going to be driving themselves in the near future, so this is a moot argument. It's simply an example of preventative crime and why I don't like it. And if you can't drink while the car is driving itself, then what's the point? You better not make laws that force someone to be sober while the car is driving itself. If anyone wants you alive, it's that robot. How else are they going to get power when they take over and build the Matrix?

The training of law enforcement also has to drastically change. I think everyone realizes that at this point. The police are trained in the same way as the military. Why? They're supposed to be peace keepers, not soldiers. If something requires deadly force, then you have special units that are trained for that, and only brought out for those instances. A regular police officer is supposed to be out there to keep the peace, not frighten the public into submission. Their only job is to prevent people from hurting each other, which includes theft. So why are they the ones out there hurting people? Why are peace officers even carrying guns? Because every American has a gun?

How about this: police are covered in full 360-degree view cameras that they can never turn off. They have their Tasers, pepper spray, and baton, but their guns are locked in the car, and only to be used in extreme circumstances. They shouldn't be walking up to vehicles, without probable cause, during a traffic stop with their weapon raised, screaming for people to keep their hands on the steering wheel. You keep cameras on them, which are their defense, and if someone harms a police officer, then it's an instant death penalty. You take the guns away from the police, except in extreme circumstances, and you take the fear away that the public has for the police, especially the black community.

Police shootings have always been out of control – they're only coming into the spotlight now because of smartphones and social media. This has to change, and it all starts with their training and what they're armed with. Also, in a society like I'm talking about, everyone is registered with their pictures on file – you get a high definition camera, with proper lighting, and you'd have to be crazy to hurt a cop that's just filmed you, especially with the direction face recognition is going. It's a death sentence. Yes, there will be crazy people out there that want that death sentence, like there is now, and the police will need to be brave.

The job needs to attract those brave enough to put themselves in the line of fire for the sake of peace. If a person has their face covered, then the officer is able to use whatever force necessary, and not go near them unless they've uncovered their face, until they've been recorded – that is their defense, not a gun.

I don't want to hear about religious practices that prohibit women from showing their faces – they can move somewhere else if they want to imprison themselves following an outdated religion. Some of those women might be happy to be forced to uncover their faces – show your feminine beauty to the world, ladies. I can guarantee that no God exists that wants to restrict your freedom of experience and ability to grow – it is only the men that created your religion who want to keep you oppressed. The women only follow these rules because they were brainwashed from childhood into thinking this is how they have to live. The brainwashing of children has no place in a free country. If it was up to me, I would create a law that treats religion like a drug, and prevents teaching religion until 18 years of age. Religion is essentially a spiritual drug for people to deal with death and attachment – it restricts their growth and search for the truth. Unfortunately, everything I just said is definitely wasted words, as none of that is going to happen. Anyway, that's it for my rant on religion.

We're never going to have a peaceful society as long as the citizens don't trust the police, and right now that's the way it seems. You should have to listen to an officer, whether he has a gun or not, because if you don't, then the penalty is going to skyrocket. How about an instant strike for disobeying an officer's orders? That is the only incentive you need, not a gun scaring the crap out of everyone, officer included. They get into this fear mode, which takes away logic, and they get an itchy trigger finger.

Would a gun make them feel more protected than the system I just described? They'd probably say yes, but I don't think it makes society feel more protected, and we're the ones they're here for. It's not us versus them. It's them working for us, enforcing the laws that we make, and how we want them enforced. They shouldn't just get to decide how to do that. If they don't like how society has decided how laws should be enforced, then they can find another job. If they've got that itchy trigger finger, and feel they need to be pulling their gun out every chance they get, then they're probably not the right people for the job anyway. Be brave, police, help create a culture of patience and tolerance, not more bloodshed.

I have a Canadian friend that went to Texas to do a firefighting course. The Americans and the Canadians were all drinking in a parking lot together, all of legal age. A police cruiser drove into the parking lot and all of the Americans ran away as fast as they could. All of the Canadians were left standing there thinking, what the hell just happened? The way Americans see the police is not the same way other developed countries see the police. They shouldn't be the enemy. Let's turn them into our friends; some of them need help because they're not very friendly right now.

I also foresee a future where everyone becomes chipped with tracking technology. I'm not advocating or rejecting this idea; I simply think it's going to happen. I believe it's inevitable because over half the population doesn't commit violent crimes. I think the majority will be happy to be able to track everyone, which would obviously just about eliminate all crimes of that nature – or at least make it easily attainable to catch whoever commits a violent crime. We can either let the current government do it, which would be horrifying towards our freedom, or we can take control of the government and dictate what kind of power this tracking chip can have in our society.

Peace officers should be controlled by the district – each district can decide on how they want to enforce laws and how many officers they need. There should also be a state task force for murders and other major crimes. Tax hunters will take care of the rest. Just kidding! Well, not really.

What about the F.B.I.? The federal government needs some sort of law enforcement, I guess. What they really need are people making sure that corruption is fought – the Inspector General being an important position, which the current president can somehow just disband when he doesn't like what they're investigating. Seems kind of pointless to even have the position if he can just do that. The C.I.A.? As far as I can tell, they're basically all about foreign affairs and messing with other governments. We won't need that.

What about the National Security Agency? It seems like their only job is spying on you. Are they trying to catch Americans from hurting their own country? Are they doing a tremendous job at that? From what I can tell, many terrorist attacks (especially by Caucasians) are advertised on social media before the person commits the crime, and they're not stopped beforehand. There are way too many people to police like this, and it's a waste of money.

This again comes down to preventative crime and how much of your taxes you want to spend on that. I personally don't believe these agencies catch a ton of people before they commit a crime. They may think they are, but how do they know the crime would actually be committed? It's a bit too MINORITY REPORT for my liking.

They're putting your tax dollars into the symptoms instead of the root of the problem. Why not spend this money to create a healthy and happy society, instead of fighting the symptoms of an unfair system? We're never ever going to completely stop crazy people from doing horrible things, no matter what we do. So, the million-dollar question is, how much are you willing to spend in taxes to reduce crimes? Because the fact is, you'll never eliminate them.

How much of your freedom and privacy are you willing to give up for security? Most people are going to be in the middle, the logical place. Some are living in pure terror and will give up everything for safety – thankfully, they are not the majority...yet. Some don't want the government anywhere near anything they're doing – they'll take care of themselves, thank you very much. I am definitely one of those people. I want complete freedom, and I'm not afraid of death. I'll take that minuscule chance that a terrorist could blow me up, instead of giving up control of communication to the government.

You take transportation every day that poses way more of a threat to your life than anything a terrorist will ever be able to accomplish; yet, you don't force roadblocks on the entire route to ensure it's safe. It's such a strange reaction that people have to terrorism when, globally, it accounts for so few deaths. You are letting them win by giving up your freedom and succumbing to fear – that's their entire goal! It doesn't matter that we've bombed the hell out of countries and displaced them all, they've already won – America has been terrorized, and we're living in fear of the boogie man.

Are you willing to give up all freedom for safety? Because we could create laws that keep every single person in their homes (we'd have to be locked up; otherwise, the crazies would still go out into other homes), and we could create safety. Is that what you're willing to sacrifice? There are dangers associated with being alive, have courage. Stop giving up your privacy and freedom for the promise of safety that can never be guaranteed. Let's focus on the root of the problems instead of the symptoms.

Be the home of the brave and land of the free. It's in the goddamn anthem! Keep repeating it to yourself if that's what it takes to remember what America is supposed to be about. It's not about giving up your freedoms and succumbing to terrorists. It's not about having trigger happy police scaring the crap out of everyone. It's not about creating a divide in the most important agency that requires trust. It's not about allowing your government to spy on you, in the hopes that they can catch someone Googling how to make a bomb. This is something which thousands of people do every day, simply for knowledge because they're curious how it works. They have no intention of ever making a bomb or hurting people, but the F.B.I. comes knocking on their door anyway (I watched an interview of a writer that this happened to).

Are you not Googling things because you're afraid the government will spy on you? I'm sure that goes through people's minds. I'm simply not convinced that any of this is making you any safer, and is, in fact, creating harm between law enforcement and the American people. That's just my opinion. You feel free to give up all the freedoms you want in exchange for perceived safety.

There's only one guarantee in life, and that is death. It will happen no matter what you do. Do you want to live a life in fear that it could happen today? Or do you want to live without fear, knowing that the universe wants you to reach your full potential, and isn't out to get you? If you ask people if they're afraid of death, many will say no, but then their actions completely conflict with what they just told you.

I once rented a room from an old Filipino man in Los Angeles. He locked up his house real tight with double deadbolts and alarms on all of the windows – no open windows allowed at night. I would walk around this neighborhood thinking, 'nobody would break in here. It wouldn't make sense.' So, I asked him, "Have you ever had anything stolen or broken into?" He bragged that 20 years in that neighborhood and nobody had been broken into. So, I asked, "Why all of the locks and security?" He replied, "There's always a first time."

This guy had had 5 heart attacks over the last few years and ate an incredibly unhealthy diet. I said to him, "You know, if you want to prevent another heart attack, you might want to eat healthier and do a little exercise." He replied, "I don't worry about that, it's in Jesus' hands." I swear to you, this is a true story and not just some fable to teach a lesson.

This is the mentality that so many people have. They don't worry about actual harm that they can prevent to their minds and bodies. This is because those harmful activities feel good and the side effects will be felt in the distant future. When it comes to things that are out of their control (if someone really wants in your house, then there's nothing you're going to be able to do about it), then they lose their logic because of unfounded fear. But isn't that in Jesus' hands as well? Why would Jesus think that it's okay to let someone break into your home if you don't lock your door, but not okay to give you diabetes and heart disease that you created?

The odds of someone breaking into your house are insignificant. The odds of you dying in a terrorist incident are almost nonexistent, before OR after 9/11. Violent crime rates are at the lowest they've been since the 1960s, yet people seem more frightened than ever. That all comes down to media and seeing rare crimes that we would normally never see. Use logic, not fear, and be brave. We're obsessed with the dramatic deaths that rarely happen when the real killer is being ignored – our own unhealthy lifestyles, which include stress and worrying about things out of our control.

Anyway, the real purpose of this section on law enforcement is to try and make you see how fear affects logic. Go out, live life, and take chances; as long as you're not living in fear, then I promise you the universe has your back. If you think bad things are going to happen to you, then that's what's going to happen. Life is going to keep teaching you these lessons until you realize that no matter what happens, you can always deal with it. And you can. Humans are incredibly adaptable and amazing...when they're not being completely illogical and stockpiling toilet paper for the apocalypse.

Chapter 9
Military and Foreign Policy

What is the purpose of a country having a military? Is it to protect itself, or is it to be able to attack other countries? What do you want your military to be used for? To liberate countries under dictatorships? Then why are there still so many dictatorships in the world? And if that's the reason, then why is America funding the largest dictatorship on earth in regards to China? None of it makes any sense. It's a for-profit industry in America, and the wealthiest people in the world are controlling legislation around it, such as defense contractors like Halliburton. From all accounts, it appears that Dick Cheney started the second war in Iraq, and guess who has his greedy little fingers all up in Halliburton's treasure chest? The big Dick, obviously.

Under the guise of liberating an oppressed society, in Iraq, and under the guise of America being in danger of weapons of mass destruction (because Saddam Hussein was one of those dictators that was tired of being rich and in control, and wanted to commit suicide by attacking America), the American government decided to liberate Iraq. What has happened now? Western oil companies are raking in the profits from one of the largest oil reserves in the world. If it seems a little fishy, it's because it is. If you don't care and you say good riddance to that dictator, then I'll agree with you. If you think there's nothing wrong with invading a country and stealing their resources, then you are an enemy to world peace.

Iraq needs to be producing their own oil if they're ever going to heal themselves and become a developed nation. And we need a real democratic nation with power in the Middle East that isn't just named Israel. The whole thing was a farce, in order to make a few individuals richer, and the American taxpayers paid for it. But the people who paid the most were the innocent lives lost in Iraq, and they're still paying under a broken system of democracy. We didn't help them at all, and it's created an ongoing war that has made few individuals rich off of taxpayer money – money that could have solved a lot of problems in the Middle East.

I honestly don't believe Americans want to spend 700 billion a year on their military. That could easily be cut in half and still be more than China (the next largest), which doesn't even spend 300 billion, despite having almost 4 times the population. They do, however, have the largest standing army at 2 million people – compared to America's 1.3 million.

So what do you think China is going to do with that military? Are they coming to invade America to take its resources? Then what? The rest of the free world stands on the sidelines and waits to see how it turns out? 'Gosh, I hope they don't come over here next.' Not a chance in hell! The free world has joined together to fight dictators in the past and will continue to do so in the future.

There is certainly a slim chance that a country is so desperate that they want to commit suicide, and they send a missile towards America. This is really the only area where military spending should be focused –

missile self-defense. Also, towards the Air Force, and I'm not just biased. If you rule your skies, then no country can invade you. Most of it, like the army, navy, tanks, guns, and personnel, can be cut back by at least half, and hopefully more.

Why would a country invade another? There's only one reason – they want the resources. Or, for religious purposes, but that's only a thing between the smaller 'insane' countries. Also, it's likely not a problem for the future. I mean, I sure hope it isn't. Can I flush some money down the toilet towards Jesus so he can guarantee that? Isn't that how it works? Although, Jesus used to be the one that wanted war and domination under His name, and Islam was the religion of peace and knowledge. The cycles in life are a funny thing.

Is there really any chance that a large, powerful nation could invade another large, powerful nation and take its resources? What would that fight look like? America invades China and faces 2,000,000 soldiers and a billion citizens who want them dead. Does that sound like a valuable proposition? What about China invading America? They get to come to a country where approximately 50 million adults own a gun, which is 25 times the number of China's military. Each soldier would have to kill 25 armed Americans without getting shot in the process. Keep your guns, it's the best defense you will ever need. However, some commonsense gun laws are coming, no matter how badly you want to fight that. No military in the world would ever dare invade America, whether you had a military or not. Not to mention that they would all have to cross an ocean to get here.

Maybe you feel the need to defend yourself against those violent Canadians and power-hungry Mexicans. If that's the case, then we better get all the troops home immediately! The American military has nothing to do with our self-defense. Satellites and nuclear weapons have turned warfare between large nations into a pointless venture. They're coming after us through the economy, and we're losing that war.

So, the reason to have a giant military must come down to the terrorists of the world – the extremists who number in the tens of thousands. The number of deaths due to terrorism is, on average, around 10,000 worldwide per year. No matter how much money we spend on the military, we will never get it down to zero. Heart disease and stroke, which can be largely preventable with a healthy diet, exercise, and stress management, kill over 15 million a year, globally. That differential becomes much greater when just referring to America. Yet, America isn't starting a war on heart disease, which could probably actually be won.

If saving American life is the ultimate goal, then why put it into a dead end like the military instead of actually saving American life? Because America is stuck in a loop. We need the military to control the world so that we can keep borrowing more money...to keep putting into the military. We also already talked about the glorious wonders of GDP. But what if America stepped down as the world police? Would China, Russia, Iran, and North Korea all of a sudden say, "The time has come! ATTACK!" What do you think? Let's play story time and take a look at how that would work out and the reasoning behind such an action.

America has stepped down from its empirical rule. They've been a celebrity now for 60 or so years, and that hard-partying lifestyle has really taken a toll on its bank account, and health. We need to work on ourselves to become the incredibly prosperous and healthy nation that we can be. It's time for a few years of detox. Now what? China and Russia want America's resources and send troops to the shores to take over America...I'm sorry, I can't even carry on with this story because it's too ludicrous and it hurts my brain. If you feel like this is a possibility, then you are completely stuck in the realm of fear, with logic abandoning all faculties of your brain. I can't believe you're reading this book, good for you!

These dictatorships want money and resources, no question, but to take over a free and powerful nation is simply not possible – even in the days when it could have happened, it still didn't work out for Germany. You're safe. Invest in actual defense, missile defense, and let the rest of the world take care of itself for a while. Pull out all troops from everywhere around the world (except for those countries that we directly destabilized) and if shit hits the fan, then the entire free world will have to come together to solve it – America can no longer be the world police and still fix itself.

As I've mentioned, new warfare is economic warfare, but there's also cyber warfare; China is winning the first, and Russia is winning the second. Russia invests a great deal into their brightest minds to train them in cyber warfare, which is why they're so skilled in hacking into our computers. At least America has that unstoppable military to go and destroy them when Russia hacks America's elections, or China owns a ton of America's treasury bonds...wait...uh oh. Does that mean America is going to attack Russia or China? What does that look like? It looks like nuclear war, and that's also extremely unlikely to happen.

By the time any country sends out nukes, the other country will have its own being sent the other way. None of these greedy overlords want nuclear winter – because then nobody makes money! The warfare of the past is no longer a viable option for making money. The supposed threat of warfare and the ability to make billions off of building military weapons is all they really care about. That being said, America should be investing at least the same amount into cyber warfare as Russia is, and be attacking them back when they attack us.

Power and punishment is now dictated by who has the most economic control, and who can create economic sanctions on other countries. If we allow China to overtake us, then they will dictate how this world functions – we will then say goodbye to the environment, to the beauty of the natural world, and to our freedom of speech. We'll also say goodbye to any chance of success, unless you're already born with the silver spoon in your mouth. Or you're willing to kneel to your leaders.

Let's be real, this spending is really only allowed by the people because of the perceived threat of terrorism. Yes, very terrifying – try to hold it together. The whole free world is in danger, and the whole free world must act to solve terrorism. But how do you fight terrorism? The 20-year war in Afghanistan has gone swimmingly well. America has decided to leave and the Taliban is supposed to take control of the country again. Wait a second...I thought America went in there to get rid of the

Taliban because they were letting Al Qaeda operate there? Yeah, maybe, who knows their hidden motives? Either way, the Taliban is a ruthless organization that is a perfect example of a dictatorship, and they don't even care about money – as long as they have enough to feed themselves and buy weapons. They only want to control the country. They want to prevent girls from going to school, and they want to prevent citizens from learning anything outside of extremist Muslim teachings. So, that 20-year war went well to liberate Afghanistan. We should keep fighting terrorism like that...NOT. In case you're really young, that was a 1990s catchphrase.

The war on terrorism is going about as well as the war on drugs, and that's because they're fighting the symptoms instead of the root of the problem. The root of the problem with terrorism is a lack of hope. These young men have nothing to do and nothing to look forward to in their lives. Guess who the most dangerous people on the planet are – bored and hopeless young men. They're the ones that fuel gang violence, they're the ones that fight the wars, and they're the ones that commit the most crimes. If you don't take care of your young men in a country, then you're going to face the hardest battles. Young men feel invincible, they want to make their mark in the world, and they feel like the world is theirs for the taking. And 10,000 years ago, it was.

They were the dominant animal. If they wanted something, they just took it. All of those years of evolution are hard to ignore. But we live in a different world. So, what do you do with them now? How do you give them something to hope for in their future? Unfortunately, it all comes down to education and skills training. You give them something to do and throw challenges at them to face. But many of these young men, populating America and the world, don't want to be educated – they want the easiest path to success, and that's usually through crime and simply taking what they want. They're going to need a lot of tough love, and some of them are certainly going to have to take another shot in their next life.

In the extremist Muslim world, the easy path means killing an infidel and getting 72 virgins in heaven. Although, I wonder if they've ever questioned the logistics of this promise? They probably try not to because this likely sounds a lot better than what their future entails in the Middle East. I read an estimate that said America spends approximately 1 million dollars to kill each terrorist. How far would that money go in helping those young men from becoming terrorists in the first place? To make them love America instead of hating us? The problem is that there's no money for those in charge in a world filled with love, or peace – only war.

The war on terror all comes down to education, especially the education of the women; because they're the ones that educate the young boys. And they're the ones that have to decide which special fellas are infected with the religion rabies...and not have their little demon spawn.

The extremist men are likely lost to this world. We're going to have to defend ourselves against them; unless we can create industries in that region, and quickly, which is certainly possible with a global concerted effort. America can't do it alone; we've done it long enough and without any sort of investment into the root of the problem. It's time to step back and re-evaluate. That doesn't mean spending the same amount on our military, or more, as Trump has done even after deciding to pull out. You're supposed to spend less and have fewer responsibilities after pulling out, that's why you do it in the first place! It's not because it feels better.

If these terrorists get strong enough, then the developed world will have to work together to fight them. In the meantime, we should be helping these countries get some industry and hope. We give them money to build schools and we defend those schools. We teach all religions, if religion must be taught, and most importantly we teach them science. We teach them that science has gotten pretty good at carbon dating, and by all scientific accounts there's no possible way in hell that the earth is 6000 years old. Since they lied to you about that, you should really start questioning everything else that they're trying to teach you about life.

Education is the way out of the mess in the Middle East – it isn't bombs and bullets. For each bomb you drop, you gain another 10 enemies for each person you kill – for every mother, sister, brother, and father that's killed by a bomb, every other family member becomes our new enemy.

You may say, but why isn't the developed world helping take care of the Middle East right now? Because they know this strategy currently being used isn't going to work. If you propose a war on education in the Middle East, I will wager that a lot of those clever European countries (that invest a lot of their money into education) would be on board with that. Maybe I'm wrong. Maybe the puppeteers don't even want them there – they want to spend as much taxpayer money as they can for as long as they can.

If the developed world doesn't want to solve this problem together, then we let those countries fester and turn into plagues for the future – deal with it then. Either way, America needs to stop spending money trying to save the world on its own, especially by fighting the symptoms through military force. It's time for rehab. The rest of the world either helps and figures out a better way to do it, or we all have bigger problems on our hands in the next 20 or 30 years. Europe has a lot more to fear from the Middle East than America does – they should be leading the charge.

One thing is certain, you have to have the people support your cause, or you will never defeat the terrorists in those countries. The citizens in Afghanistan do not trust America because the soldiers treat them like they're all terrorists. But just leaving Afghanistan at this point would be irresponsible. Fortunately, they have very large deposits of lithium that they can mine. America should invest in the infrastructure to make this happen, only employ citizens of Afghanistan to do it, and make sure all of that money goes to the people. You give the young men, who aren't infected with religion rabies, something to defend and fight for. This would end up being much cheaper than continually fighting the symptoms of terrorism.

Do you think we're safer and better off by letting western oil companies take money and resources away from Iraqis? We need to support these countries in building the infrastructure necessary to produce their own oil and mine their own resources. We need to help them build schools, to teach the truth of the world and the universe (not just what the

Koran tells them), and we need to defend those schools. The extremist young men are likely lost to this world...unless we build industries for them to work in. Still, can a person infected with the religious rabies ever be cured? How many of them can be cured? I don't know the answer, but it's probably not a good one. I hope I'm wrong. And if a terrorist wants to leave their organization in order to work in these industries, then we should let them. Extend the olive branch and give them a chance.

We empower the average citizen in these countries to protect themselves, and they will eventually defeat the enemy for us. You think the average Middle Eastern citizen wants constant war and control over their lives by dictators and terrorist organizations? They want freedom, like everyone else in the world, and they want world peace. But sometimes peace has to be fought for. So, give them the weapons and training to fight for themselves. The whole world needs to contribute towards this, not just American tax dollars.

Let's forget about terrorism and go to the real heart of America's military, and that's control over the world. Does the average American actually want military control over the world? For what purpose? So that we can make whatever legislation we want? So that if someone pisses us off, then we can bomb them without any sort of retaliation? So that we can invade small dictatorships that don't have any allies and steal their resources? Do you want a guaranteed future collapse? Because as we already know from our earlier history lesson, all empires fall. Maybe you don't give a shit because you'll likely be dead upon the collapse of American society. Okay, boomer! That was me trying to be young and hip.

I honestly don't think the majority of Americans want military control over the world. If they do it's because they don't understand that the real power comes through the economy. Either way, they're not given a choice. You're too stupid to know what's good for you – that's what a typical politician will say, in nicer terms, if you try to tell them you want direct democracy. Granted, there are likely a ton of messes that will have to be cleaned up because of the intricacies in government that we won't be able to foresee. So what? We're already paying for government mess after mess without any sort of progress in sight – we're going backward!

What does it look like to decrease the military? To abandon all bases around the world and say, 'you're on your own for a while.' This is what I think it looks like: we give those bases, and all the weapons and machines in them, to our allies. We have a base there because they're our ally, so treat them like an ally, and trust them to continue to be our ally. What other choice do they have?

The free world is the world to be in; it's not the dictatorship world. Dictatorships are lonely countries with allies that are all only thinking of themselves, and citizens that are ready to revolt at any instant. The free world is united – it is united under a common interest of freedom and peace. It has the strongest economy. No country will ever be successful in the new world unless they're part of the free world.

It's not so complicated to be a part of the free world, either; all you truly need is freedom of the press. Not all dictatorships have to be evil, but

I can guarantee that if they're restricting freedom of the press, then they're doing evil things. Remember, freedom of the press means that any journalist can come into your country and report on whatever they want, unharmed. Would you trust Russia if they said, 'no, no, no, we are now free country. We have fair election. Putin is supreme leader again. Everyone want that. And journalists report all okay.' I hope you did that in a Russian accent. But no, that wouldn't quite cut it. We would need free journalists going in and doing their amazing journalist work – being the unsung heroes that they are, who fight corruption and unearth government atrocities. See, it's not so complicated.

Unfortunately, it will be incredibly hard for those countries to topple their dictators. Sorry, that's their problem. We can't go in and liberate a country with force. How could it even happen? They would end up losing more innocent lives with us bombing them than they would if they united, stopped working, and demanded a free country. Yes, their military will kill some of them. You don't quit. Freedom is worth it. America had to do it.

Plus, they will likely be in pretty rough condition when the free world no longer does any sort of business with dictatorships. Those governments won't be able to feed or pay their militaries. The citizens won't be able to travel. Eventually, everyone will get fed up. Or fed down...you see what I did there? They'll want to join the free world as well. And what is a dictator without their military? They're dead is what they are.

But these people will be cut off from the internet and they won't know the truth of what's happening – only what their state TV is telling them...that the rest of the world is the enemy. So, we fly drones, 35,000 feet in the air, and drop information pamphlets into their countries; old school style. The drones will likely then be shot down. There's no way the government can stop these pamphlets from getting into people's hands. I have a feeling that there are hundreds of millions of people in China who are ready for a revolution – those who are at the bottom with absolutely no chance of ever increasing their station under a dictatorship. They could very well be trying right now and we would have no idea because of the lack of free press. I think we'll just need to pour gasoline on those smoldering embers and show them that we support them. All you have to do is spread the truth. The people will take over from there, eventually.

Let's be honest, the reason America deals with dictatorships in the first place is because of resources, specifically oil. But oil will be a thing of the past in 10 to 20 years when we get hooked on that pure, uncut hydrogen. So, let's not even talk about oil.

The real problem will be silicon. China mines and produces more than half of the silicon in the world. Guess what silicon is used for? Solar panels and computer chips – it's kind of important. But guess what? Anyone can mine silicon. You can make silicon from sand and coal. You can get it from quartz. This is an easy solution. Forget about silicon – I bet you were really worried about China and silicon before I mentioned it. They also mine a lot of minerals and metals that we use. But we've already talked about this in the chapter on resources – we absolutely need to become independent and harvest all of the resources that we need ourselves. Whatever it costs to make this happen will be worth it – there is no future imaginable that looks promising with China controlling the production of crucial resources.

What else does China give us that we absolutely need? They buy a lot of soybeans from farmers. How many people do you think the farming industry actually employs with the way giant mono-crops are farmed? The entire farming industry employs a little over 1% of actual farmers. And the soybean industry is subsidized, meaning that taxpayers basically pay for these giant corporations to make money off of China. How much do you think these corporations pay in taxes? I actually don't know because I don't care. I know it'll never be enough to validate feeding a powerful dictatorship.

China makes a lot of our stuff – if you want America's economy to get stronger, then producing our own products is obviously the way to go. You just may have to spend a bit more money. But that money is going back into your own economy, which should increase wages, and not to the economy of a dictatorship superpower. World peace is going to come at a cost – as they say, 'freedom ain't free.'

China offers absolutely nothing that America, or the free world, needs. There's nothing that we can't prepare for, anyway. We can't get off that addictive China white tomorrow, but we should certainly be preparing to wage economic warfare on them until they free their people.

Similarly, Russia also has nothing to offer America, besides beautiful women. I sure do love those Russian women, though. It would be a real shame to not have them giving me that evil eye, that they do so well, whenever I try and hit on them. But I'm willing to sacrifice, in the short term (I couldn't go long without that), to force them to get their freedom. Saudi Arabia? Forget them. They're not part of the new world, and I can't imagine how many decades it's going to take to get freedom there. Iran? The young people there are pretty much already starting their democratic revolution. I have a feeling they'll be allowed in the new world. North Korea – give them the pamphlets and wait a few decades. Besides, China is the one keeping them going, and once China gets freedom, then North Korea falls.

The rest of the countries are insignificant in terms of safety to the free world. And, as I've said, even if all of those countries combined, they would not stand a chance against a united free world. Large militaries are a thing of the past. It's time to adapt or die.

So, we decrease military spending, but what about all of these jobs 'lost' because of military cutbacks? Do we really need to go there? After all of the industries that I've said are going to need tons of new government workers in order to heal America? Come on, let's face it, who would be better at being personal trainers than ex-military members? They would probably be happier doing it too. I think personal trainer jobs should be first and foremost reserved for military personnel who lose their positions, to give them peace of mind – the last thing we want are angry young men losing their careers and having nothing to look forward to. If they want to do something else, then we train them. They're first in line. And they can always be a part of the reserve force.

Second in line are other government workers who lose their jobs because of efficiency – there are a ton of government workers and they need to be on board with direct democracy, or getting the numbers will be more difficult. They're already going to be hard to sway because they feel comfortable and secure with this system that largely benefits them.

GDP wouldn't change. Government spending will likely be more, but the salaries these men and women make will be going towards creating a better America. To actually protecting America from the disastrous future of our own making: with China owning our treasury (that's money), Medicare collapsing from an obesity epidemic, and a wasteland due to irresponsible farming and mining practices. Not to mention a civil war with the poor that results in martial law, and that results in losing all of our freedom. The real enemy is not without, it's within. Stop feeding them!

What about the actual military that we'll be paying? If we're not sending them to other countries to fight, then what will they be doing? This whole COVID-19 thing has inspired an idea. We train hundreds of thousands of military members to give emergency aid. By that, I mean be able to insert needles, give fluids, take vitals, and have a general understanding of healthcare. All they do is train anyway; why not train them in something that America is going to need during the next pandemic. Because let me tell you, these diseases aren't going to stop. They're going to keep getting bigger and meaner the older and sicker our population gets. It's nature doing its job. Since I highly doubt humans are just going to let nature do its job, as we haven't been able to do that yet, we're going to need to come up with better solutions than shutting the world down every 10 years.

So, we get these military members Hazmat suits, and they go from home to home of the sick and tend to them. I don't think I need to say that we also need to stockpile medical equipment for these future pandemics, and you have to assume that the government will learn their lesson after this. If a person is healthy and unafraid of the disease, then they should be able to carry on with life. If a person is vulnerable or afraid of getting sick, then they can quarantine themselves, with social assistance. To shut the whole world down again is simply not a solution going forward. We're going to see the decades' long effects that this will have on the economy, all to save people who were near death anyway. Not to mention, most elderly people don't even seem concerned about it – they're the ones that just want to carry on with regular life! Yes, healthy people die from it as well, but it can't be that much more dangerous than regular life.

What choice did some governments give their citizens in deciding whether they wanted to risk their lives or not? Zero choices. Furthermore, they're barely going to help those whose lives they just destroyed. It's bullshit and it's not democracy – they control our lives and tell us what to do. They protect us from ourselves! I personally want no part in a nanny state that no longer thinks for itself.

The most confusing part is that they pick and choose what's dangerous and what's safe, and their choices make no sense. I want to go back to heart disease, even though there are many other examples. Almost 700,000 people die a year from heart disease in America. COVID19 has a death rate of about 1%, which I think is an overestimation. I caught

COVID in February of 2020 and it really wasn't a big deal – a few days of a weird feeling in my lungs. I think we're going to find that a lot more people have had it than they are predicting. Either way, if everyone in America caught the virus, then we're looking at about 3 million dead, and then it's done. That's a little over 4 years of what heart disease would kill. Except heart disease isn't going to stop killing. So, are they making laws that force people to eat healthy and exercise in order to save American life? So why are they making laws to protect us from this virus that will kill, in the long run, way fewer people than heart disease? Because they don't think in the long term, only the next election – they don't plan for the future, they only react to the present.

Furthermore, most of the people that die from the virus would likely die within the next 5 to 10 years anyway, either from old age or simply being unhealthy. Governments are destroying millions of livelihoods, which is a huge factor in mental health, in order to save people who could be healthy and unscathed by this virus, but have chosen not to be through many years of poor diet and no exercise.

They say it was to prevent the healthcare industry from collapsing, and instead collapsed almost every other industry in the process. That's why the military should be used for home care, to protect hospitals in the next pandemic.

I'll admit, I might be a bit too right-wing to give advice on disease, due to a great immune system from a healthy lifestyle and stress management (meaning I don't worry about things out of my control). I've never sanitized anything in my life and rarely wash my hands – I invite germs into my body at all times and almost never get sick. I've never had the flu or had a fever in my life. I've never taken pills to mask the symptoms any time that I've ever had a cold, which usually last for a few days. I let my body deal with it naturally and now my immune system is as strong as it can be. Again, people take pills to mask the symptoms, they cheat to lessen the suffering, and that balance has to be paid somewhere – as in weakening your immune system.

Sanitizing the world and running from germs weakens the immune system and is going to end up killing a lot of people in the long run. A healthy immune system and healthy population are the only real defenses against future pandemics, so let's focus on the root of the problem instead of the symptoms.

The military could also be used for catastrophe relief – they build houses after hurricanes and floods. I believe they're already used for this when shit really hits the fan, but this should be their main job. What are they actually defending against right now? People like to say the military defends their democracy and their freedom, but who is trying to take your freedom? Your own government! Anyway, I think those are pretty good uses for the military. Let's let democracy decide instead of greedy politicians, who only care about political contributions and the next election.

Before I end this chapter, I need someone to please tell me the logistics behind the 72 virgins in heaven. Maybe I'll blow myself up to get me some of that. But I want 72 experienced professionals, no question. Then again, are they even real women or just sex robots that God has created? I think it's safe to say that there aren't 72 virgins for each and every sadistic psychopath out there that wants to kill infidels. But we do have that many virgin sex robots here on earth for them instead. That would certainly be a cheaper solution than fighting them. Also, are we allowed to specify what we want and get assurances before the blowup part? I would certainly need assurances that it's going to grow back before my penis blows apart. That means scientific proof; otherwise, why take that chance? I'd rather settle for virgin sex robots here on earth. Come on, terrorists, think about it – they're still in the box and guaranteed never opened! That's more than you can say for those robot 'virgins' God will create. Who knows where they've been!?

Chapter 10
Immigration, Overpopulation, and Social Assistance

There's an idea going around that open borders would help the world. I've read some of the arguments and it would certainly help the developing world in the quickest fashion, but I don't think the developed world would take too kindly to it – judging by how many countries are reacting to immigration right now. If you're wondering why there's a sudden rise in anti-immigration, it's because immigration rates have risen substantially in the last 20 years.

In the 1970s, the percentage of foreign-born citizens in America was around 5% – it's now over 15%. Citizens of countries in Europe and America don't seem to like that too much. You can call them racist all you like, but when people feel the culture of their country is under siege, they react with fear and hate. I would imagine that if China, Africa, India, or the Latin countries all of a sudden saw different races creating entire cities, where they didn't speak their language, and wanted to keep their own culture, then they would react the same way.

Denmark has created an interesting law that doesn't allow immigrants to form communities – they have to disperse among the general population in order to learn and adopt Danish culture. If a person wants to immigrate to another country, they should adopt the culture of that country, shouldn't they? That's really the only way to stop the rise in anti-immigration groups, which are only going to grow and become more dangerous if nothing changes. They could likely become the terrorists of the future. I think immigration should go back to around 5%. The people who are currently on social assistance should be doing a lot of the jobs that immigrants typically do. Any sort of immigration that's based on bringing in skilled workers should be refocused into training our own citizens to do those jobs. This decrease in immigration may not be logistically sound, especially with baby boomers about to cost a fortune in healthcare. But with a healthier elderly population, I'm hoping the costs can be manageable. I could very well be wrong in this regard. Those poor countries are going to face tough times, but America needs to fix itself before tackling those problems. It's the same idea as putting on your own mask in an airplane before helping the person beside you.

I also don't think America, at this point, should kick any immigrants out. But they absolutely need to register. If they're making under $20,000, then they won't need to pay taxes, but they still need to register. After 5 years of working, they can become a citizen, like they can now. If they can't maintain steady work in those 5 years, then they should be kicked out. I don't think America can afford it, and I don't think the citizens want to pay for social assistance for an influx of immigrants. Maybe some states will. I guess we'll find out when they get direct democracy.

States should be allowed to decide their own immigration policies. If a state decides they want and need more immigration, then they should be able to make their own laws dictating that – not unlike the way it is now. An immigrant has to register upon arrival in America, and they have to stay in the state (or states) that allow extra immigration. After 5 years of working and becoming a citizen, they should be allowed the same benefits everyone else receives, including skills training, education, and healthcare. I also don't think a non-citizen should be able to buy land or property. Housing markets around the world are being driven up by Chinese, and then the citizens of a country can no longer afford to buy property – that doesn't sound right.

New Zealand passed a law that prevents non-residents from buying property – I personally really like that law. It doesn't mean that foreigners can't eventually buy land or a home; they simply need to become a resident first. I actually think that it should change to become a citizen first. To allow the Chinese to buy up the world, and not even live in these houses, is not going to turn out well in the future. Let the Chinese invest in their own country – they've just made a fortune off of slave labor, and now they're going to abandon the people that made them that money? Not even invest that money back into their own economy and help their country prosper? I don't think so. I get that they don't want to live in China because it's a prison. So use that wealth to fight the government and start your own revolution. Don't run away like a bunch of cowards.

If an immigrant commits a crime, then they should be immediately deported. Not spend a year or two in detention (waiting for a trial), put in prison, and then deported. That's a bit ridiculous if you ask me. If an immigrant keeps coming back after they've been kicked out, then they get the 3 strikes and you're out treatment. As I said, America needs to fix itself before it can worry about fixing other countries. A healthy planet is dependent on a healthy America – immigration will have to wait a while. Besides, ending the war on drugs will start the process of healing Central and South America. Here's another Article for you:

Article VIII: Every citizen/resident, or those wishing to become a citizen/resident of the United States of America shall be registered with the government; in order to vote, pay taxes, and/or receive government assistance. Not registering will result in deportation, heavy fines, and/or jail time.

There's no question that the greatest problem facing mankind, and planet earth, is overpopulation. As technology gets better, we'll likely be able to at least create a population that can survive...for a time. The problem then comes down to the natural world. The main problem there would be some very overpopulated Asian countries, who seem less interested in the natural world than developed nations do. That's simply a function of their struggle for survival. If you disagree with me, it's likely because you've never been to Asia. Most people simply don't care about the environment when they're struggling to survive themselves.

So what happens to the natural world during this long struggle for survival, before technology is able to ease the burdens, and the balance between the rich and poor becomes more stable? A lot of destruction, most likely. I'm not going to sugar-coat it. There is no quick solution to this problem.

Nature will continually try to fix this problem for us with diseases that kill the old and the sick. We're likely going to fight those diseases with every fiber of our being. Perhaps a path exists that is full of a right-wing population that follows the rules of survival of the fittest – but we're definitely not on that path. Besides, even if the deadliest disease in history comes and wipes out a billion people – which would likely cause global chaos that would take decades to heal – that still wouldn't solve the problem of there being too many humans.

If we could create a global society that limited the black holes, those that refuse to contribute (I'm not talking about those that can't contribute), and limit the amount of children people can have, then it would certainly ease the burden. But to get the overpopulated countries on board with any sort of policy like that would entail mass genocide, and that's simply not going to fly with this population.

I feel like there's only one option: slow it down as best as possible and ride this upward spike until it starts coming back down. It's inevitable that a decrease in the population comes at some point – nothing in nature is able to just keep rising without coming back down. All species on the planet follow the same cyclical pattern of up and then down – humans will follow this same pattern. It's a law of nature that we're not going to break. The goal is to flatten the curve as much as possible and create balance as quickly as possible. The most healthy and stable species are those that don't participate in the giant swings between up and down. Can we create that? Most certainly. The question is, how many millennia will it take to do so?

There is surely a path that humans can take in which we slow the upward trajectory and then slow the downward trajectory, in a controlled and intelligent manner, without any sort of catastrophic loss of life. How likely is that to happen? Not very, but it exists. To go on that path would take great sacrifice and foresight – not something this population full of selfish and greedy, one cookie eaters is known for. Forget the choice of two cookies in an hour; it would more likely be five cookies in a decade. How many children on earth would take that offer? How many adults? Perhaps the next generations, who are growing up in the information age, will be better equipped to enact the changes necessary to create a stable population. Only time will tell.

I believe there's only one way to slow the upward trajectory of population growth and that's through education. A common theme in this book, I know. More specifically, the education of women and young girls, another common theme. There's no arguing that an educated woman has fewer children than an uneducated one – so follow that theme. It's going to take an incredible investment into poor countries to do this; the already stable and educated populations of the developed world are going to have to come together to share the financial burden. It's in all of our long-term best interests – something politicians seem to care nothing about.

It can't be that difficult to teach birth control methods to girls in the developing world. We need to hammer home the idea that it's okay to wait until their late 20s or 30s to have children. That God doesn't care if they have sex before marriage, as long as they do so responsibly.

Or, teach them that it's okay to not have any children at all –

studies show that there's zero difference in happiness levels between people with children and people without. Society tries to teach us that the way to a happy life is to get a stable job, buy a house, own a bunch of stuff, and have children. That's simply the way to keep an unbalanced capitalistic society functioning, which requires constant growth. It's not the only way to a happy life or a sustainable population, and in many cases it's exactly the opposite. We need to slow down how many children women have by increasing education, giving access to free birth control, and access to free abortions – simple as that.

In the developed world, most adults are typically only having one child or less per person. I actually think that's a sustainable ratio, even with people living longer. As the population becomes more educated, they will become more focused on their own growth instead of the idea that a family is what you need to be happy.

Unfortunately, the poor and uneducated are having more than one child per person. If it seems like a recipe for disaster to have humans who can't support their offspring having the most offspring of anyone, then you're a very clever individual. So, how do we stop people who can't afford to raise children from having children in the first place? Well, we can do that with the most controversial idea in this book.

I'm going to reiterate this because I don't think the readers who are ruled by compassion (feminine energy) will be able to get past this: with direct democracy, you will have the choice to decide whether you want to increase your taxes to pay for these people, or if you want to make the hard choices in order to create a balanced society in the most efficient manner. To do this as quickly as possible, it's going to take the most drastic actions in order to correct the imbalances we are seeing. If we had tackled this problem sooner, or if the baby boomers never existed, then we wouldn't have to take such drastic actions.

My idea is simply to not allow women to have children if they're on social assistance. They can wait until they're a functioning member of society to do that. With the social assistance programs implemented today, a woman can have as many children as she pleases and collects more and more money with each child that she has; albeit, it's not very much. In fact, it's not really enough to care for a child properly.

Some of these women are taking advantage of the system and are using that money on alcohol and drugs. Why else would a woman want to keep having more and more children that she can't afford to raise? These children grow up neglected, and the only path they see to survival is to take advantage of the system themselves. If they want to get ahead, then they sell drugs, become prostitutes, or they steal – they eat other people's cookies because they weren't even given the other option.

That part is not controversial – many people would agree with what I just said. The controversy stems from the question of how do you really stop a woman from having children? Do you sterilize her before she has any children? That doesn't sound right. What happens when she becomes a functioning member of society and has the ability to raise a child without government assistance? We can't sterilize them before they've done anything wrong. However, what about if she's already had three children and is on government assistance? I say absolutely you do.

Immediately. If you disagree, then you can raise your taxes to pay for these people. Right now, we are going into debt to pay for these programs and that will become against the law with direct democracy.

There's a myth in America about the reduction in crime that took place in the 1980s. Government officials, at the time, attributed it to a hard stance on crime, even though studies showed that this didn't have any effect. What reduced crime? Roe vs. Wade – the legalization of abortion. All of those children that would have grown up in toxic environments were no longer around to commit crimes.

So, do you do forced abortions? I personally don't have the slightest problem with abortion. If a woman or a couple isn't ready to have children, then they should have that right to wait, or never have them. It doesn't make sense to not allow abortions in an age of overpopulation. If humans were on the brink of extinction, then perhaps you make abortion illegal for the sake of our species, but that's obviously not the case now. But forced abortions are a completely different ballgame, and just talking about this idea is going to inflame a large portion of the populace. Remember, this is simply a discussion of ideas.

Do you enact forced adoptions? Rip a baby away from its mother and stick it with another family? To force a woman to even go through pregnancy just to lose the child seems like a form of torture. Not to mention the problems that adopted children statistically face in society; such as depression, lower success in school, and higher drug usage. I'm not on board with that.

How about this: a woman on social assistance is pregnant with her FIRST child. She has the choice between aborting, putting the child up for adoption, or keeping the child. After having that child, and keeping it, she can no longer have any others – sterilization. Why was she getting pregnant when she was on social assistance? They should be given all of the free birth control they will ever need and be knowledgeable of the rules. You give her the choice of what she wants to do. After she has the child, she gets a year to look after it, and then the process begins to make them self-sufficient.

My idea is to have these single mothers take turns in looking after children. Let's say they each look after 5 children of other single mothers for a year, that's their government service, and then they go through the skills training program. We put cameras in these facilities or homes to prevent abuse, and this is the agreement they make in order to have this child. Some of these women may really enjoy this job and are good at it. Thus, the job then becomes their new government job.

For the women on social assistance that already have multiple children and they're pregnant? Forced abortion or forced adoption (their choice). Sorry, but what the hell are you doing with your life? Use some birth control!

If they're on social assistance and they already have children, then they should be getting trained to join the workforce, or they're going to lose their social assistance...and their children. If they want to commit crimes, then you already know what I think should be done with them. Their kids can be looked after by those mothers I just talked about who want, and are good at, that job. To allow a mother on social assistance to stay home, simply to look after a few of her children, is not efficient. A dedicated facility could look after many more children while those mothers join the workforce. If they don't make enough to pay for daycare, then it should be subsidized. It would still be considerably cheaper in the long run than allowing these mothers to do nothing, and raise children that see that as an option for their own lives.

If a woman is already in the process of getting trained and educated and gets pregnant, then it would be pretty tough to tell her that she's not able to look after her child. Or, if she's highly motivated to make her life better for the sake of her children, as my mom did, then it would also be very difficult to enforce any such policies. Therefore, an investment into more social workers will be necessary in order to make those judgment calls.

These women who already have kids should also be forced to take a birth control shot, or get an IUD, in order to prevent any more pregnancies while on social assistance...or just instantly sterilize them. I mean, how many kids should people be allowed to have? Especially those people who aren't in a position to raise kids. They are affecting other life on this planet by creating future criminals, and by asking others to look after them – that's now against the law. Personally, I'd like to see a world where everyone is allowed one child – not one child per couple, but one child per person.

If you have a child while in a relationship, and you break up, then you can still have another child with someone else who hasn't had a child yet – everyone gets one. There are a lot of details to work through with an idea like this, and I'm not going to get into it because it's so many decades away from ever being close to being implemented in the free world, that I'm not even going to go there. It's an encroachment into freedom that is simply too controversial to tackle until it becomes very clear that we need to address it. People in the developed world, who are already paying their way, are not having ridiculous amounts of children and asking for government assistance, so it's not really an issue anyway. The issue is the giant black holes that these social assistance junkies are creating with each passing generation. That can't go on.

Maybe you're on the far left, and you simply can't bring yourself to enact any sort of policy like this. I'd love to hear your ideas on how to enforce a sustainable solution. I really would love to hear ideas. Unfortunately, I don't think you'll have any. The only thought going through your head will be, 'oh my God, that's horrific! I can't do that. There must be another way.' And then silence. I personally don't consider that an acceptable argument. If you're incapable of making hard choices, yet have no other solutions to offer, then you don't really have the right to tell others they aren't allowed to make those hard choices for you.

If you're willing to pay the extra taxes to let these people continue on this path, then, by all means vote for that. Hopefully, you're in a community of like minded individuals that all share your sentiments, and you can all raise your taxes to support this cycle. That's not creating balance and therefore you'll have to correct that balance with sacrifice, as in sacrificing your money. It's your choice in a democratic society –

continuing to go into more and more debt, however, should not be a choice of a democratic society.

Do you think, right now, a taxpayer can say, "No, I don't want to pay for someone to raise a child that has no intention of ever taking care of it herself?" They can't, but they should because that's infringing on someone else's life. To have children and expect society to look after them is simply not a recipe for long-term survival. Politicians will never tackle this problem because it's too controversial.

I'm pretty sure politicians have nightmares about having to take a stance on controversial issues – they skirt the subjects and give a bunch of platitudes that mean nothing. Their only objective in life is to keep their heads down, not get noticed for anything that will ignite either the far left or far right, and do just enough to get re-elected. The system is flawed right down to the roots. Only the people, through the majority, will ever be able to take on these problems. If too many people want to keep their heads in the sand, which is called being an ostrich (and is worse than being a sheep, because they're smarter than the sheep and should know better), then our future is going to be very grim.

I am well aware that I'm going to be attacked by the far left over what I just suggested; as well as the 3-strike proposal. Both the far left and the far right are going to object to a lot of things I say in this book – don't worry about them. They are imbalanced and illogical. It is the majority, who are in the middle, that must create a better future. Those two other sides, combined, may make up the majority. But they will never join forces because they are diametrically opposed in every way. Don't worry about their loud squawking – they are not the majority.

I suppose I have a ruthless stance on this subject, and that's because I've seen it firsthand on many different levels. I've grown up in poverty-stricken communities where the perceived way to survive is to have as many children as possible, and collect assistance for each new child. My father also collected assistance his whole life, despite there being hundreds of jobs that he could have done. Instead, the government gave him money to do nothing. I've also seen my mom use that system of assistance to get trained in a job, and was then able to support her children on her own. She had two children, which is a sane amount. What about if she had five? How would she have ever gotten out of that hole, raising that many children herself? Why would a woman ever let herself get to that point?

The fact that governments allow this to happen is just another example of why they shouldn't be allowed complete control over policies and our money. They're holding the credit card, but they get to just party for a few years and then pass the card onto someone else. The interest gets paid by the average American who was never given a choice. It's an insane system.

You may say, 'where is the man's responsibility in all of this?' That's a very good question. If the man is working, then they should have to pay, absolutely. Maybe a man who's on social assistance has already had children that he's not paying for – I think it's pretty clear this man needs some immediate sterilization. That should also go towards men who are not on social assistance, yet aren't paying child support either.

A man might say, 'why is it only her choice to keep the child? I didn't want to have a child.' Which is also a very valid point – where is the man's right in all of this? Well, what did he do to prevent pregnancy? Did he ejaculate in the woman? Then he's lost all rights – sorry, you're a moron. Even if she says she's on birth control, whether it's a lie or not, you should never ejaculate in a woman if you're not ready for the consequences. What if the man did everything imaginable to prevent pregnancy? Should he be forced to give up his life for that freak accident? I personally don't think so – a responsible man should have some say.

So, how do you prove that the man did everything possible to prevent pregnancy? Record the whole thing? Highly unlikely and against the law...for now. Get her to sign a waiver? Hey, now we might be onto something. The problem is, most guys have just given everything they've got to get a woman into bed; you think he's going to jeopardize that with a waiver to sign? Not unless he's rich or extremely good looking. Sorry, guys, this is a tough one.

I'm open to hearing solutions. Otherwise, you're taking the chance when you have sex that you could be giving up your free life. Men know it and they still take the chance. It's that good of a cookie. The terrorists should try it. Oh wait, what would it be like having them impregnate thousands of women and then taking off? I take it back, terrorists, it might be better just to blow yourselves up – sex robots in heaven can't get pregnant. Although, can you have kids in heaven? I bet they'd say yes. So, if it's all the same, then what's the point of being on earth? My head hurts.

What if the woman has a one-night stand and doesn't know how to find the man? Or know his last name? Or he lies to her? That responsibility kind of has to fall on the woman, doesn't it? She's the one that has to carry the burden of birthing a child, so it becomes her responsibility to not sleep with a man unless she knows how to find him. If she doesn't care, then she can have an abortion, no big deal.

If we could eliminate religious brainwashing in this regard, then it probably would no longer be an issue. Why they want 20 billion humans on the planet seems a bit counter-intuitive. Oh wait, they then get to brainwash those little monsters, who then give them 10% of their wages (that's a real thing if you didn't know), and I guess it starts to make more sense why abortion among religious teachings exists at all.

Teaching young humans that they should have a bunch of children because that's what God wants is a form of genocide and should be illegal. To tell young girls that they can't use birth control because God doesn't want that is genocide and should be illegal. The woman should always be given a choice, and so should the taxpayers who have to pay for it.

Another very controversial topic to discuss is gestation testing – as in testing the fetus for potential disabilities. I doubt many people are going to agree with me on this, but I believe that it should be a law to have prenatal testing. If there's a chance, a certain percentage, that the child will have mental or physical disabilities, then the parents have to decide whether they want to have, and pay for, that child.

Obviously, there are no guarantees, and there should be a safety net for accidents. However, I don't believe it's society's responsibility, in this technological age when we can determine beforehand for a lot of disabilities, to be raising, or at least given a choice in raising, these humans. Humans that will never contribute in any way, and will cost an incredible amount of resources to live a life with almost zero growth. That should be the responsibility of the parents, if they choose to have that child.

I once dated a woman who looked after a mentally disabled man whose parents had given him up to the government to look after. This grown man had the mind of a 2-year-old and would become violent. He had 3 full-time workers looking after him, and only him, for the entirety of his life. This is not a rare occurrence. It cost almost $200,000 a year for this individual, which obviously equates to millions over a lifetime. That money could have raised countless families out of poverty. She even thought it was insane, but hey, a job is a job.

I'm sorry, far left-wingers, but you don't get to just have all of the good in life without any sacrifice. Of course, the most amazing option would be to just give everyone everything they could ever possibly need in life. But you know life doesn't work that way. At least not yet.

Right now, the government pays for all of these programs because they're afraid to tackle them. It also raises GDP, which allows them to borrow more anyway. If you want to save everyone, then you're going to have to pay for it, pay a lot for it. Right now, the government is going into extreme debt that is going to collapse society in the future. We seem to think that there doesn't have to be a sacrifice to take care of those that nature would normally eliminate. If you want to take care of them, then raise your taxes. People should still be given that choice, and the majority can decide what they want to do – that's democracy.

What we're living in right now is a leaky dam patched up with duct tape. Duct tape is strong, but it's not going to hold a dam that's about to burst. Instead of sacrificing the few, when we had the chance, just about everyone is going to drown. It just likely won't be in your lifetime. If that's how you care to live your life, by not making any hard choices because it's simply too painful, and to let the next generations face incredible hardships because of your cowardice, then, by all means, do your best to create that Band-Aid society. You'll pay for it eventually; in heaven, hell, or in another life, whatever you believe in. If you don't believe in anything, then you're probably already on board with the hard choices that have to be made. Or else you're completely selfish and don't care about anything but yourself. Is that the majority? God, I sure hope not.

If you're a young person that's going to have to pay for this in the future, then you better start thinking about the hard choices you're going to have to make, and other possible solutions. Soon, you'll have the numbers to correct the problems that this population refuses to address. And if you don't, then watch Mad Max a few hundred times and get a bunch of training on how to survive in a post-apocalyptic world. But don't get a car that runs on gasoline, like they all did. Get an ostrich to ride around on, it'll be ironic...and I know young people just love irony.

Change is coming, you can decide whether it's two cookies later, or one cookie now and eat one human later...actually, you'll probably have to eat a bunch of humans. The first one will definitely be the toughest...and most chewy...but you'll get better at cooking human flesh, don't worry about that part. Wow, fear mongering is fun! Now I know why media outlets love it!

Chapter 11
Entertainment and the Future

This is an area that is very near and dear to my heart; specifically, the film and television industries. I'm not sure if you've noticed, but the film industry is kind of broken. It's the golden age of television and streaming; because they've adapted and haven't been stuck in the same formula. The film industry has become like the current government, and streaming has become what we want to create – an exciting new future full of limitless possibilities.

We've already talked about the future of jobs – most of them are going to go to robots. Making lifelike sex robots will probably become the biggest industry in the world – start investing. People are going to become more and more afraid to touch each other, with each passing pandemic, and we're going to become more and more isolated, with technology to keep us company. I see this as the evolution our species has to go through until we accept that the risk of death is part of living a full life; sad, I know.

There's one area that robots and artificial intelligence will never defeat humans, and that's creativity. The best jobs of the future, if they're not already the best jobs of today, are going to be in the creative fields. Artificial intelligence will never be able to create something completely unique. Let me clarify that. I don't mean they won't be able to come up with new ideas. What I mean is that they'll only be able to take what's already been done, and improve or alter it in some way. They will never be able to come up with something that's never been touched upon before.

Machines are not connected to the collective conscious, and if you don't believe in that, it's because you've never thought about it. Everyone has experienced it, like when you think about someone and they call or message. Scientists have even proven the existence of it with bonobos in Japan (a type of ape). You can research that yourself if you're interested. The point is that machines don't have a soul to connect to this dimension of thought, where creative frequencies come from.

Entertainment and the creative fields are going to have to take up a great deal of jobs that are lost to robots in the coming future. Many people living today want to have a creative job that pays the bills, but it's an incredibly competitive and cutthroat way to make a living. The majority gives up and settles for that nursing or engineering job...or, God forbid, that government administrative job.

Another major problem with creative jobs is that there are a ton of middlemen that take profits away from the artists. I'm not sure if I've mentioned, or if you could ascertain on your own, but I hate middlemen. They typically create inefficiency and take profits away from those that actually deserve the reward. The position of being a middleman also doesn't typically create a ton of jobs, so it wouldn't be destroying an important industry. Technology almost always gives us the opportunity to get rid of the middleman...like we'll be doing with the government.

Imagine a future where there is a lot of unemployment – probably not that hard to imagine. Robots have taken 60% of traditional jobs, and a lot of people are on the government payroll, doing random things like cleaning public spaces and whatnot. We're going to need to get rid of these middlemen and spread the wealth among more artists, to create more jobs. Right now, a successful artist makes an insane amount of money. Are they that much more talented than anyone else? Absolutely not. There are millions of incredibly talented people out there, they just either lacked the drive and ambition, or didn't get that stroke of luck that so many successful artists got.

The first thing we need to do is allow children and teenagers to really explore their creative sides; this is our one major advantage over the robots, and over China. We should invest heavily in this. Those that want to pursue a path in the arts and entertainment industry will have to do their year of government service, like anyone else. That is unless they're already making money in high school from their creative pursuits, and then they don't need further training. If they think they have the ability already, then they should go for it.

So, how do we get rid of the middleman? Netflix is great; I think most people will agree on that. Spotify is also amazing. Anyone older knows how much we used to pay to listen to music and watch movies – this has streamlined the process with efficiency, and it's helped the audience out in a big way. But they're still taking massive profits away from the artists that truly deserve it. I'd like to see the entertainment industry find a balance between capitalism and socialism, like every other industry.

Imagine a future where the middleman no longer takes huge profits from artists. Instead, we all pay 1% in taxes to pay the actual artists, which, for the average person, would be about $250 a year. Right now, if you're paying for it, a Netflix and Spotify account would cost roughly the same. But they're taking more than half of the profits. They innovated and created a great service. Thanks a lot, guys. But that money needs to be spread out more, in a future of balance between capitalism and socialism. I suggest having these two top companies still manage these services and receive 1% of our 1% to be our middleman. This would still be an incredible profit for them, especially since Netflix will no longer need to invest in their own materials.

How the artists would get paid would be the model that Spotify uses...not Netflix, theirs is terrible. Netflix pays a film or series an agreed-upon amount, and it doesn't matter how much that show is streamed...although, they may have bonuses, I'm not exactly sure. Either way, Spotify's model is much better: they pay the artists a direct percentage based on how much their music has been streamed – the better your music, the more you get paid. You should be able to download anything from this service, watch or listen whenever you please, and it's all tracked – in order to pay those artists a percentage of your taxes. It should be run on a file sharing platform, in which everyone transfers files to each other, so that we don't need to create servers the size of Texas.

Everything an artist makes will come down to how well they're able to market their material, and how good that material is. This is where marketers and investors come in. Remember, there is likely no more stock

market, so wealthy individuals will have to find other areas to invest in –
this would be one. An artist still has to find these people to invest in them,
not unlike now, but without Wall Street in the picture, these rich
individuals should be more eager to gamble in this industry.

So, we've now created a platform that has all media on it – movies,
television series, news networks, music, books (which are a bit more
complicated in terms of profit-sharing), short films, skits, games, etc.
Anybody has access to any of it, and those artists all make a percentage of
your taxes depending on how much you watch, listen to, play, or read their
material – all getting divvied up every month and paid directly to the
artists...or their management companies/investors. To clarify about books:
this platform should have a service to print books, if someone doesn't want
the e-book, like Amazon currently does. A person can pay what it costs to
print a book and ship it, and then the author simply gets paid like it's a
completed e-book – the average time it takes a person to read the book.

If an artist is great at marketing and was able to produce something
really cheap, then they have an opportunity to get rich without any other
help. This will be the American Dream of the future. I guess it's already
happening with YouTube. But why give that company so much money
that could be going to the artists? This system of distribution would also
help combat pirating, since everyone would already be paying for the
service.

What about people who are making under $20,000 and not paying
taxes? How about we give them this one for free? Life is already likely
quite difficult for them. Or, maybe if they can't pay, then everything has

ads – just like Spotify's model.

Any other countries that want to adopt the same model, with similar tax rates, can put their material on the same platform, and their taxes are spread out the same way. If a country doesn't do this, then individuals from anywhere in the world can pay $30 a month to subscribe to it. Anyone from around the world can put material on this platform, but they only receive a share of the foreign subscriptions. The price these foreign artists pay to be on this platform is to give free access of their product to Americans. The idea here is to subsidize American artists with tax dollars, not to give that tax money to foreign artists. There should still be a lot of money to be made simply from foreign subscriptions.

Of course, there would be an incredible amount of material for individuals to sift through on a platform like this. Word of mouth will be a big factor, as well as reviewers that you come to trust. Also, algorithms that pick out what it thinks you'll like, the same as these companies use now. The possibilities on how this could work are endless – the main point is to reduce the demand for the middleman as much as possible, and spread the wealth among as many artists as we can. There will still be some that make many hundreds of millions, or even billions, but I'm hoping that we can develop a system in which the wealth is spread out. I predict, in a system like this, both the top and bottom artists will make more money.

There should still be theaters because some movies are meant to be seen on the big screen. That's where big Hollywood studios will still come into play – I don't want to bite the hand that potentially feeds me.

Although, I'm really hoping I won't have to depend on them, and that will all depend on you. The majority of films will be seen at home, as it is now. Theaters are dying – they make their money on big-budget, special-effects-driven movies. I see no path in that changing, and many theaters are going to go under. But Hollywood will still invest in giant productions that belong in theaters, and some will live on.

Even if an artist only makes $20,000 or $30,000 a year, I can guarantee you that they'll be happy because they'll be following a creative pursuit. The happier you are in life, the less materialistic stuff you need. Nothing creates a happy and healthy life more than having creative freedom in your job; unless you're one of those creative people who lose their minds. But that's part of the balance – there has to be risk involved with something so lucrative and appealing.

Anyway, that's my idea for a way to spread wealth among artists of the future. This doesn't apply to photographers, women showing their asses on Instagram, or hands-on artists like painters etc. – they'll still have to do what they're doing now and sell their assets. In closing of this chapter, I'd like to share with you my own experience in trying to break into the film industry, before we get to the final chapter – how we create direct democracy.

I wrote my first screenplay at the beginning of 2014, after never really contemplating a career as a writer. At least, not any more than the average person who probably thinks it would be a pretty swell job. I wrote a sex comedy that I thought was the most unique and creative story I had ever seen. I was certain that within a few months, I would be making this film with major stars – specific ones I had in mind that had to be in this movie: Seth Rogen and James Franco, to be exact. I knew absolutely nothing about the industry. I thought there would be pathways for writers to submit their scripts to be read by studios. That is, inexplicably, not the case. They will not accept anything that isn't either asked for or given by a top tier agent – even if a writer is willing to pay a reader.

I submitted this script to a site that claims to be able to get your script read, if you can score very high ratings from their readers, which, of course, you pay for – that's fair. However, even if you can get these high ratings, chances are incredibly slim that anyone is going to buy your script and make it. The odds of selling a speculative script (something you wrote on your own, without being paid to do) are less than getting hit by lightning. Hollywood would rather pay a few writers, throw them in a room to write a premise they're given (likely something that's already been done), they come up with some regurgitated, formulaic garbage, and that's the Hollywood film industry. They would rather pay professional writers to write shit they have no passion for, than to actually read something that a spec writer has put their heart and soul into. It's really strange, and it's the reason why you keep seeing the same ideas and the same formula played over and over again.

Anyway, the very first rating I got on this site was 1 out of 10. I thought that maybe one meant it was the best it could be, and 10 was the worst – creative blindness is a funny thing. It didn't make any sense. I read their comments, and I didn't know what they meant. That's because I didn't realize there was a formula that movies have to follow – since I didn't have any education in screenwriting, I just wrote what I wanted to see on the screen.

These professional readers reject anything that's outside of this formula. Any movie you see that doesn't follow the formula, such as any Richard Linklater movie (like DAZED AND CONFUSED), is because they made it themselves. Quentin Tarantino would have also never made it past these readers if he hadn't made his own connections. What typically happens is, these people make their first film, which becomes successful, and then Hollywood funds them to make more...even though they're not following the formula. But they had to somehow manage to do that first one on their own, which obviously limits a ton of great stories.

I paid an executive 'in the know' a few hundred dollars to read my script and have a phone conversation with me. He was really excited. He said he loved the script – it was hilarious, unique, and highly creative. I was like, 'that's what I've been saying all along!' He then went on to say that nobody would make this film and that I was going to have to make it myself. It didn't follow any of the rules that Hollywood requires, and I was a nobody. I didn't believe that could possibly be true and completely ignored him.

I spent the next 10 months learning what the silly formula was and trying to get anyone to respond to me – not a single person ever responded to an email. But nothing was going to stop me – I had ideas on how to change the world, and the film industry was my ticket to the spotlight to share those ideas.

My next script was a sci-fi, and it didn't follow the formula either. I knew it didn't, I just wanted to write it. I didn't try to get anyone to read that, it just had to get out of my head. The next two scripts I wrote, I made sure I followed the formula. I then won a small competition with a low budget drama. I was sure that this was my ticket in. Why would a producer not read a script that had made it through all of these different readers, and that had been deemed to be the best? Still nothing.

The film and television industry has a closed-door policy. It's an incredibly lucrative place, and they don't want it getting flooded with a bunch of strangers. They're greedy, like most humans, and don't want to share the wealth. Therefore, it's all about who you know that can get you in the door. Not only that, but the readers, who essentially make or break a writer's career, also have very little incentive to even read a script. They get paid less than $20 an hour to read script after script and give feedback. If the script is good or bad, it really makes no difference in their lives. They skim through them, usually struggling writers themselves, and often miss important parts of the story. They have no incentive. I instantly thought of ways to solve this problem.

I wrote more scripts and a book about my life, which, if you've gotten this far into this book, then you might as well read that one too. But I warn you, it is sexually graphic, crude, and offensive to most readers. If you start it, then you have to promise yourself to finish it. The point is not where I began but where I end up. The point is about forgiving people for their mistakes, as well as forgiving yourself for your own. It's about finding purpose in life. About how people fill a void with different addictions, some healthier than others – mine was sex. It will make you think about life differently. And, above all, it's a comedy. So, remember to laugh and not get so uptight about those that I make fun of. I make fun of myself more than anyone. Anyway, I won another, bigger competition with a historical drama I wrote about a slave ship, which has placed in just about every competition it's been in. It's the type of movie that could be in the Oscars. Still, nobody will respond to me. I can't even get a manager, let alone an agent.

Then, I won a competition with a low budget comedy I wrote called NO POLITICS. The point of that competition (called 'your script produced') is to actually produce the winning scripts, which is similar to an idea I'd already had, which I'll describe next. I was in the pre-production stage and COVID-19 hit. Now, here I am writing this book instead. We're all caught up. Let's get to my ideas on making money.

Imagine a studio that produces a film a week – low budget films that focus on good, unique stories instead of explosions and superheroes. A writer pays a reader of this production company $70 to read their script, which is on the cheap side of what they're charged now to simply get feedback, with no opportunities to actually do anything with the script. The reader gets $65 of that (which I guarantee is more than any of them are making now), and the other $5 goes towards running the website that handles this process.

The reader then picks the best script they've read that week, and it goes up the ladder. The next level has 7 readers – more established producers or agents that have an eye for good scripts, and aren't afraid of reading. Each one of those 7 then picks the best script out of everything they received that week, and it goes up to the top, me. I read one script a day and pick one every week to make for less than 5 million dollars – that's only for production costs, not actors, writers, music, or any of the talent.

If a reader finds a script that is made, then they are given a small percentage of what the film makes. They are incentivized to not only find the best scripts, but to also work with the writers to make their scripts better. They're able to talk back and forth: the reader loves the story but wants a couple things changed before they send it up the pipeline. The writer agrees, rewrites, and sends it back to that reader. The production company doesn't have to pay for any of this, as the writer is paying; which they'll gladly do.

The reader gets 1% of the profits if their script is made, and the writer gets 3%. The next person up the ladder gets 1% as well, and also has the same opportunity to speak with that writer about improving certain aspects of the story – that's 5% of the net profits to find and pay for amazing scripts.

These movies are then put out for free. If a viewer likes it, then they can easily donate a dollar or two, either on the website (fundyourrevolution.com, which I've already bought...can you believe it was available in the year 2020?), or by texting a number displayed at the end of the film. This production company is purely non-profit, and a large part of its existence is to bring energy and water to Africa.

Everyone involved in the film, including the actors, writer, director, music, etc. make 45% of the profits (after the production costs are paid off), 50% goes towards world causes, and 5% goes towards increasing the budget on the next film. Everyone makes a percentage (some of them negotiable, like with the actors, and some of them set, like with the production crew, writer and readers), and nobody is given a set amount of money before the film is made. I would like to create all of my business dealings in this way – it's how you create the most incentive for people to do the best job.

This production company would fund a brand name called FUYORE – fund your revolution. We would invest a million dollars in companies with amazing products that just need an infusion of cash and marketing to take off – like Shark Tank does but focused purely on philanthropy. These companies would then give 20% gross, in perpetuity, from the products they're selling, into various avenues. We will set up branches in various parts of the world to fund a democratic revolution towards direct democracy. This obviously only works for products with large profit margins.

When a person sees this brand name, FUYORE, on a product, they'll know that 20% of their money is going to whatever we're working on at the time, instead of to a greedy corporation. I hopefully won't be working on energy forever – those energy plants should be able to fund the production of more plants once they get running. There are lots of problems in the world to solve. This will be a never-ending challenge for me. But I need money, and influence, to do most of it.

Anyway, I thought I should share a couple of my ideas on how to make money, before we get into how to create direct democracy in America and the world. Now we get to your job...it's so easy you won't even believe it.

Chapter 12
How We Get There

To do everything in this book likely seems impossible to most of you. Even just getting direct democracy probably seems insurmountable. At every suggestion you probably thought to yourself, 'they'll never let that happen,' or, 'this guy is going to get killed.' If we unite, quickly and in large numbers, then there's nothing they could possibly do to stop us. If you take your time and wait until there is no other choice, then it will be much harder to make changes.

If you're worried about me getting killed, don't. It's the last thing I'm worried about – death is easy, life is hard. Life doesn't just give you the easy way out. If that's not good enough for you, and you constantly tell yourself that this guy is going to get killed before anything happens, then that is the path you will go on. I'm not going to experience that path, because I'll be dead, so I wish you luck on that journey. Your job still remains the same whether I'm in your world or not.

Make no mistake, by releasing this book I just made enemies with all of the most powerful people on the planet – the drug cartels are really the only ones who operate without fear. The dictatorships of the world will likely want me silenced as well, and they're pretty ruthless. The others are cowards, controlled by fear of losing their wealth. They will all hide in the shadows until they have no other choice than to come out and strike; fortunately, by then, I won't matter and their efforts will be pointless.

In fact, any efforts to kill me become pointless once this book reaches a million people – that's the arbitrary number I've set for the tipping point. You may think a million people is quite a lot for a book to achieve, or not enough, in this age of non-readers. In reality, getting to a million will be quite easy, and would only take a few months, as long as everyone does their job.

Your job is to get THREE people to read this book. How hard will that be? Probably harder than you think. Most people hate reading. You're one of the amazing ones. Trust me, I'm a writer and even getting my closest friends to read anything is a nightmare. But you only have to get three people to do it. There's also an audiobook. If you know an influencer, then go after them, hard. Then, the responsibility gets passed onto them. Keep hounding them until they read it – they're lazy and they won't want to. It's your only job.

With the money from this book, I'm going to fund my political comedy movie myself, and I'm going to put it out for free. Maybe I'll make a documentary based on this book instead. Hopefully, I have enough social media followers that it works and makes money. I'm also going to build a generator that works off of pressure differential – I can't see how it wouldn't be a perpetual motion machine. I hope it can solve some energy problems. I realize that came a bit out of left field, but this idea has been bugging me to get out for many years. When an idea won't leave me alone, it's usually a good one. Not to mention, I finally received the last piece to the puzzle just a couple weeks before publishing this book, so that has to mean something. After I do all of that, I make more movies. I've got some decent ones, I promise.

After the first few are released, and they make money, we'll open it up to all the other desperate writers out there with amazing stories – there are thousands of amazing ones. I know that because I have good scripts, and they would sometimes only make the quarterfinals of competitions. I would say to myself, 'where the hell are all of these great movies? Why isn't Hollywood making them?' I don't think that those executives, who make the decisions on which movies get made, even know what a good script looks like – they're businessmen trying to do a job that belongs to a creative. Regardless, if they don't want those scripts, then we'll be happy to take them.

And then what? And then the message of direct democracy spreads. I'll be out there doing everything I can to spread these ideas. I have parts in movies for myself, that will be easy to pull off. My goal is to get in the spotlight as much as I can and preach direct democracy. Unfortunately, that's all I can do. In case you didn't know, or haven't figured it out, I'm not American – I'm Canadian. Your worried little brother to the North, if you didn't know where Canada is. That's a joke aimed at Americans and their ambivalence to global geography.

Here's a joke *aboot* Canada: Why did the crazy Canadian try and start a political revolution in America? Crazy Canadian: 'Why not? What else do I have to do up here?' I guess that wasn't my best material. But seriously, life is just a game to try and make the best possible life you can for yourself and everyone around you. America is around me. And America is the most important country on this planet.

America invented the culture that I will never live without – a culture of freedom and possibility. America invented everything that everyone loves. And I love America! But you can do better, let's be honest. I'm worried for you. I'm worried for Canada (because whatever happens to you, happens to us), and I'm worried for the world.

America is not the only country not doing all they can – every single country in the world needs to step up their game. When I talk about the inefficiency of government, I'm often referring to my experience with Canada's government. Canada has a higher per capita debt than America does. We need direct democracy as much as anyone! Everyone's doing a shit job – some better than others. The ideas in this book pertain to every democratic nation on earth. I simply focused on America here because of the power they wield to make global change.

The best way to get a message out to the world is through America. They may think that nobody is watching and nobody cares about American politics; in reality, the majority of the world pays more attention to their government than to their own. It's like a messed up reality show where all life on earth is at stake – doesn't get any more addicting than that! They can start this democratic revolution towards a goal of world peace. They've started just about everything else that's awesome in this world. America means everything if we're to attain world peace in the next 100 years.

As for my own selfish reasons: I believe Canada and America are essentially one country – whatever happens to America, greatly affects Canada. What happens in Canada doesn't mean a damn thing to America, and that's why there aren't Americans telling Canadians how to fix our mess – we have plenty of our own messes that direct democracy would solve. Not only that, but we are also all living on this planet together, and we all want world peace. When I continually say 'we' in this book when referring to America, it's because I believe it is 'we' – not just 'you.' Anyway, that's the reason the crazy Canadian is doing this. But all of that doesn't really fit in my terrible joke. Sorry. You can put that sorry in a Canadian accent if it tickles your fancy.

So, let's look at the story of how this all happens. You've done your job, the message is spread, and there's a buzz about this idea of changing government structure. But it's insane, are you kidding me? That's a massive undertaking, and the economy would collapse in the process. Wouldn't it? It sure would, if you tried to do it all at once.

This is what I see happening: in two to four years, the idea has spread to enough people, especially the younger generations who will likely be all over this. Many will probably disagree with a lot of what I suggest, but the only idea in this book that matters is direct democracy. You can call it real democracy or true democracy; however, I'd rather you didn't call it true democracy since I don't want people to think this was my idea (True is my last name, if you didn't already know).

I had never heard anyone talk about this, but it's the definition of democracy. Maybe one day, democracy will evolve to just thinking of your vote, and that's it. This is simply the evolution of democracy that can exist right now. And I didn't invent democracy. I've also recently heard others speaking of this idea, it just hasn't gotten into the mainstream. Once it does, there won't be any stopping it.

So, the idea has spread. Now, someone needs to start a third party in America running on an entire platform of direct democracy – that's their only policy. I can't do it, I'm Canadian. This probably seems like the most difficult part to you, but it's really not. I wish I could do it, but foreigners aren't allowed to donate to political contributions or run for office. I'm allowed to spread ideas there, and I'm allowed to find Americans who want this. I can also help unite them under one umbrella. You will have to fund them and create them. I wouldn't worry about the right people stepping up to run in your district or state; that will be inevitable, as long as you do your job and spread these ideas to enough people. And it's going to take at least a few congressional elections.

What I see happening is a few very capable individuals run in progressive districts. They are eloquent, passionate, and can argue their points extremely well. They drive their three fossilized opponents into the ground. The direct democracy party has won 3 seats in the House of Representatives, and nothing in the Senate, sad. You now have three 'spies' among the enemy to show you exactly what these congresspeople are doing, and how the whole shit-show works.

They will have a team that reads every bill that goes to the House. They will dissect it and put it online for people to easily understand. The average person can't read a bill – bills are full of gibberish and legal terms. They're written to dissuade people from actually reading them. Even most congress members don't read them – they simply vote along party lines, which is how they're able to sneak laws like the Patriot Act in there. But we're going to see all of the nonsense. There will be an app/website set up so people can vote on these bills.

Anyone from around the country can vote on these bills; because your vote doesn't mean anything, yet. It's just a bit of practice to work out the kinks in the voting app. Although, if the House votes were very close between the other two teams, then it's quite possible that this party could be the deciding factor. Then, what people in these districts vote for on bills would actually matter. How exciting would that be? The voter inputs in their own income and the app does everything else for them: showing how the bills would affect their taxes (if the system wasn't built around ambivalence towards debt), the pros and cons of what they're suggesting, and get a good idea of how the whole process works.

These first elected officials will still have the same job that normal congress members have, which could be seen as a problem since they don't have any experience. But what do you think these congressmen and women are really doing on a day to day basis? Do you think they're actually figuring out the details of how to run their districts? Or, are they mostly focused on talking to those that can help them get re-elected in two years? I've heard them in interviews, after they've retired of course, saying that they spent half of their time trying to get donations!

The middle managers in those districts already know what needs to be done and how to do it – let them do their job. Yes, these freshmen will have to make decisions, but they'll be commonsense issues. Congress members running and winning in other districts aren't special in any way, besides being good at public speaking and having a strong desire to be in political office. I assure you, the district will still function with someone who has never done this job before – it happens all of the time with new candidates. Hopefully, we can get a few experienced congressmen and women that see the validity of this model and want to switch teams – vote for them, they already know how the broken system works and will likely have ideas on how to fix it.

There are approximately 230,000,000 people of voting age in America – 20% of those people are likely never going out to vote, no matter what's going on. That leaves about 185,000,000. In the 2016 election, almost 125,000,000 people voted – 62 million for each party. I'm not going to talk about the 2020 election that broke records for voter turnout, because that was mostly driven by a dislike for the opponent more than excitement for their candidate. That's obviously not how a healthy democracy should work.

What are the odds that these people abandon their teams? I would say we'd be lucky to get 20% from each side, which would equal about 25 million. You'd likely need at least 70 million people to take over Congress, which is about 31% of the voting population. I honestly believe 31% of people will be on board with direct democracy. But, we need to get those people who normally aren't involved to vote for this system.

You have to remember, it's not just getting the majority of seats out of the three parties – you have to have more seats than both of those parties combined. They're going to vote together to block any sort of legislation for direct democracy. It will be the first bipartisan thing they truly make love over. And then they'll go back to their stalemate of not getting anything done.

You need 51% of Congress, which is the way it should be. You need 218 of the 435 congressional seats and 51 out of the 100 senate seats. Ideally, we need ⅔ of all seats in Congress to have complete control over the Constitution, but that's likely not possible at the start, so workarounds will be necessary. Just getting the majority will be a huge win and giant step towards real democracy. At the very least, we can allow online voting for future elections, and that would likely spell the end for the other two parties. They know that, which is why they never talk about online voting.

There are approximately 138,000,000 people in America between the ages of 20 and 49. You would need only 51% of this demographic to vote for direct democracy, and you wouldn't need the older generations. These are also the people who don't show up to vote because they don't see the point – they'll see the point now. The below 49 demographic outnumbers all other generations. These are the younger half of Generation X, Millennials, and Generation Z. They aren't afraid of technology, less afraid of change, and are online most of the time anyway.

They'll still be afraid of change and it'll be the job of the level-heads to talk rationally to them. Get them to sources of information like this book, if you can't convey the ideas adequately. But, you don't really need 51%, because there are plenty of people in the older generations who are fed up with either party, and will be hungry for change as well. I don't see this number being insurmountable. It is going to be difficult and is going to take funding as well as the right people for representation.

Funding shouldn't cost a fortune for this movement, since it will mostly be spread by social media, organically. Still, if those 70 million people each put in $8 towards this party, then that would equate to a little over a million dollars for each and every seat in Congress. Then, you go to your last ever vote that you'd have to stand in line for. I don't know if that's enough incentive to get the young out to the booths, but if it's not, then it will be eventually. As the younger kids grow up with this idea, it will seem less frightening to them, and we'll eventually have the numbers.

From the very get-go, the media and everyone in charge will never stop fear-mongering about how this would never work. The economy would collapse, you'd be invaded, the Kool-Aid man will bust through your wall. Nah, they wouldn't say that – people would like that. But they're going to spread a fear campaign like they've never done before. It won't matter, you know their games. You're going to have voices of reason speaking out for these ideas and countering their arguments.

I will go on every platform I can to debate these people. But most networks likely won't put me on. This is a social media campaign. You don't need to watch the state-run network of Fox News or any of the other fear campaigns out there. This is a major leap, and one that is unprecedented. Be brave and take the leap of faith.

They're also going to say that everything I suggest in here would cost too much and isn't possible. Keep in mind, they'll be using current models of how an inefficient government works. If a society did everything in this book, which includes some very drastic right-wing actions, to balance out the left-wing policies, then I truly believe we could create a wealthy country that's not going more into debt. But the odds of any country doing ALL of the things I suggest in this book, within the next 50 years, is very slim. I hope I'm pleasantly surprised. We just do what we can do and we'll learn what's working and what's not as we go. I just can't imagine how it could get worse.

No matter what happens, you can always go back to those other parties once you get the laws in place for direct democracy. However, they'll never again have the power like they do now. You put in laws that allow you to immediately alter what they do if you don't like what they've done. If they try to remove those laws, then you know what you have to do – vote them out again.

Let's go back to when this party is about to take control and the next steps after that. It's been 6 to 10 years since these ideas went mainstream – you've had multiple representatives in the House and the Senate. Hopefully, we've even had control of a state or two and were actually able to make some real changes in legislation. The rest of the country then sees that this is working. At the very least, we should have had enough seats to get things done with either the Democrats or Republicans – this is how other countries usually operate who aren't stuck in a two-party system. You side with another party and you each get something done that you want. It's not this tragic comedy playing out between two parties who are unwilling to compromise. So, you've hopefully been getting things done in the government. You think you have the numbers and now make your move for control. You put everything you have into the next presidential election and you take over Congress.

You don't have to do anything else. Relax, take a breath.

Let the economy and the stock market settle. The stock market is going to crash, big time, and it might not come back. In fact, it'll likely crash before the election and this is going to really scare a lot of voters. We must keep a level head and know that this is expected. The companies that are most affected will likely be companies that wouldn't have survived under this new system anyway. Other industries will start booming and the stock market will hopefully settle into a more balanced and sustainable position. No matter what, at some point the stock market is going to fail whether we introduce a new government or not. The most important step here is taking care of those that have lost their retirement funds.

We need to make it very clear that if anyone takes their money out of the stock market, then they won't be protected against their losses. After 4 years, if the stock market hasn't recovered, then we reimburse what people lost on their original 401k investment. We'll be creating a more safe and secure retirement fund anyway, they won't need the volatile stock market or investments that depend on constant economic growth. We're building a balanced and strong economy that won't take part in the unpredictable swings that this unsustainable system creates.

The media and the other two parties are going to plead with people that they're all about to die – they're going to say that the economy is going to tank like never before. But not much changes. Life goes on as usual in America. The GDP will likely go down with the stock market, but that's okay. We're not going to borrow money from banks or other countries ever again. The only future debt we're going to incur is publicly owned debt, through loans to your people – you gamble on yourselves.

The only thing that's really happened with the stock market is a bunch of rich people left an illegal poker game, because some crazy asshole showed up saying the cops are on the way. Nothing has happened to money or the economy in America. Some incredibly wealthy people will have just become wealthy people. So what? If publicly traded companies need help, then we give them low interest loans. They use the stock market as an indicator of how the economy is doing, but it is not the economy. When the rich get squirrely and take all of their money out of the game, the economy doesn't just collapse. The two are not directly connected.

Either way, they just left that one game. They're still in America, doing business, and trying to make money. If they leave America, without an incredibly good reason (besides I'm scared or I don't want to pay taxes), then you ban them from doing business in America. If they make equipment or technology that other businesses use, then you ban the companies that do business with them as well, until they find someone else to use. Nobody important is going to leave America and the profits that you bring them.

Then, we start making changes. The first action is to pass a law that allows the citizens of America to create legislation and decide where their taxes go – The Direct Democracy Act. If we can't figure out a way to make this work within the Constitution, then those elected officials will have to be your middlemen...how inefficient. You'll have to vote in a president who signs off on that bill. If you have the numbers to take over

Congress, then there would be no question that you have the numbers to vote in a president. This position would likely be best for someone who has worked in politics for a while, and wants nothing more than for America to have direct democracy – they will exist, I assure you.

For instance, someone like Bernie Sanders; although, he'll likely be too old by then...maybe, maybe not. There are others like him, don't worry. They are there to simply sign that first bill, and decisions on laws and policies are no longer in their hands. They can guide Americans to what they think is best, but that's it. They become the ambassador to the world for America, and they will give updates on anything of federal importance.

Since districts will be mostly controlling themselves, the federal government's job will be pretty straight forward – the military, disaster management, foreign policy, and to spread the wealth and resources between states. There are many other tasks this person will have to do as well. This job is still incredibly important, and you want somebody very competent, who isn't simply a narcissistic con man. But in this new system, sociopaths like Trump wouldn't last very long. Plus, they wouldn't be attracted to the position in the first place, because they would no longer be the leader of the free world. They're simply a manager and ambassador.

Your next job is to make a law that takes power away from the Federal Reserve and eliminates any debt that you owe them. Let them take you to court, you make the laws now. Although, as I've mentioned multiple times, we're going to have to create laws and policies that follow the Constitution – this has to be a completely democratic and lawful transition. As far as I can tell, there's nothing in the Constitution that talks about a centralized bank, so we don't need 66% control of Congress to do this.

The FED won't need to tell you when you can print more money. They're like the prison and healthcare system – they want you to keep coming back, in this case to borrow more money, without ever solving the root of the problem. You're going to need to create more money at the start. The value of the American dollar is going to go down, no question. Likely by no more than 30 - 40%, which it has done before and will do again, and the world doesn't end.

You've got some investments to make into your country and it's going to take a lot of money to do that. You can't just get this money without some sort of balance towards the negative – that's the sacrifice you have to make. Your dollar will lose strength, but don't worry it'll come back. If we do this right, then it'll be stronger and more stable than ever; 10 years down the line, when you've paid off your foreign debt using the money from your vast resources, and nearly everyone is contributing with either tax dollars or their labor, you'll have a bullet proof economy. You have to trust that you can correct that downturn and not panic. If America doesn't act, then that downturn is going to come eventually, but without any hope of it ever turning around for anyone but those already at the top.

China creates all the money it needs, in the form of very low interest loans, in order to fund the incredible infrastructure projects they're doing. We will need to do the same thing if we want to compete with them.

We can't go crazy with printing money. Any money created for infrastructure has to go towards industries that will provide a sustainable and independent income; such as investing in renewable energy, altering factories and energy plants to trap emissions (they sell the CO2), altering sewage plants to grow bio-fuel or recycle water, and buying the equipment and land to drill and mine for resources – as well as many other money-making infrastructure projects.

Infrastructure involving things like roads and bridges has to be paid for by taxes, because these investments will never create a return on investment...unless you create tolls. Wages for government projects should also be paid for through taxes, as much as possible. What you're already spending in this regard shouldn't change, we're simply rearranging where wasted money is going in the current system.

We need to release people who are in prison for non-violent crimes, put that $40,000 a year, that you're already spending, towards a wage, and get them working on projects to fix America and the environment. Teach them the skills to do this work, because infrastructure and environmental projects are going to take up a large portion of new jobs. Many of these jobs will be labor intensive and best suited for the young – we're going to have to put our blood and sweat into fixing our countries. The older individuals we release should be trained in the less physical jobs. As these young workers age, they should then be transferred over to the less demanding jobs as well.

The majority of money you create for infrastructure can't be going directly into people's pockets, it should mostly go towards the actual cost of equipment and supplies – in order to stem inflation. As long as the money you create is mostly going into the actual materials for these projects, then you should be able to create as much as you need and it won't affect inflation. That money will be trapped in inanimate objects – it shouldn't need to be paid back until all other debt is paid off.

There will be profit made by the companies that supply equipment and materials, so we have to work with businesses that are willing to take the least amount of profit, and that profit is something we will have to pay back as soon as possible. Still, this shouldn't create noticeable inflation. You must use tax income, as much as possible, for anything that's going directly back into the economy, when it comes to infrastructure.

Giving government loans also shouldn't affect long-term inflation, because that money will be coming back...eventually. Therefore, we can give trillions out in loans in order to build all of the infrastructure needed to fix the environment and become truly independent. We allow capable individuals to run government projects (with production incentives), or else give interest-free loans to build renewable energy power plants, bio-plastic factories, sustainable farms, carbon sequestering equipment (that will have to go on many factories), hydrogen plants, bio-fuel farms, synthetic fuel plants, insect and inland fish farms...the list could go on. If it takes these industries 50 to 100 years to pay off these loans, then so what? They will be helping the environment and creating a ton of jobs.

As long as these new industries can at least break even, then you've just boosted your economy – not hindered it with inflation. But always remember this – the income tax these workers contribute must be used to pay off those loans, before that money goes towards anything else. The FED prints trillions to bail out banks because of unsustainable practices, and they give that money to people who are already rich. They also don't have any semblance of a plan on how to pay it back. So why can't we print money to put into infrastructure projects that create independent income, jobs and help the environment? It doesn't make any sense. Maybe I'm missing something but this shouldn't affect long-term inflation too much.

Another area where you can print money, that shouldn't create too much long-term inflation, is preventative healthcare. Once people are sick, that has to be paid for by tax income. Preventative healthcare is an investment into your future, by keeping workers healthy and paying taxes, instead of draining the economy by constantly being sick. This would include the fight against obesity. Once healthcare costs start going down, you keep the same budget and you use that surplus to pay for preventative healthcare. Eventually, that cost should start going down as well, and then you pay off those loans using that budget surplus.

Investment into preventative healthcare is likely a 60 year plan and would have the most impact on inflation, because it will take the longest to see a return on investment. The upside being you've got a healthy population that can fight off future pandemics – how many trillions would that save? That might be worth losing a bit of short-term strength in your dollar. A key point I want to make is that you must always work towards paying off that public debt – whatever you print has to always be public debt. Except now we won't be paying hundreds of billions on interest to world banks, foreign countries, or the FED. If this affects the world using the American dollar as the global reserve currency, then let them use something else – that would have zero impact on the average person.

Anything to do with education and skills training is another place that's an investment into your future, and you can create money for. When people start working, after being educated or trained, then we pay off what we invested in them through their tax income, before this income is used for anything else. That's how all of these loans get paid off – through the income taxes collected from the jobs created. If you want your economy to really become impenetrable, then eventually all government spending has to come directly from taxation, and not loans. That will take time.

This current strategy of creating just enough money to keep the system afloat, without ever making the large investment to actually fix the root of the problem, is not a good long-term strategy. The major downfall to what I suggest is that the dollar will lose strength for a period of time. And, of course, the wealthy will lose some of their wealth...if that's a downfall to you.

Be warned: if you print too much money, and put it towards dead-ends that will never repay that debt, then America turns into Venezuela. That will be another fear campaign that they will turn into one of their greatest hits. The difference is that we're doing this to get rid of corruption – all of that happened to Venezuela because corruption was out of control, with no way for the people to fight it. The same thing that happened in socialist Venezuela is happening in America, simply on the other extreme towards capitalism. The result will be the same if nothing is done.

Most importantly, you need to create balance between right and left with the hard decisions, as I talk about regarding healthcare, prison and social assistance. Otherwise, this system will never go into the positive – you'll always be sinking more and more money into people that don't deserve it, or else be paying a fortune in taxes. Or, worst outcome of all, you don't pay extra taxes for the left-wing policies you enact, you print unlimited money to pay for this unbalanced ideology, and you completely make your dollar worthless. Definitely don't do that. Always remember the balance. Here's the most important Article for you, and it pertains to printing money.

Article IX: The government shall only be able to create money for loans, education/skills training, preventative healthcare, resource extraction, low-income housing, natural disasters, pandemics, and infrastructure projects that will create sustainable income. All other government spending must come from tax income. Collecting foreign debt is forbidden. Furthermore, all income tax produced from these investments, excluding resources, must be used to pay off said investments before that income tax can be used anywhere else. Income tax produced from resources must be used to pay off foreign debt before that money goes towards public debt. Federal taxes must be raised by an amount that pays off expenditures into natural disasters or pandemics within 5 years.

That last bit is an agreement that the country makes to share the cost when natural disasters affect certain areas. Federal taxes would not have to go up by much to pay for these events. This is the last fun with math that we're going to have, I promise. The tax income should be at least 4 trillion dollars with everyone contributing and no write-offs – it's now around 3.3 trillion. To pay off a 4 billion dollar catastrophe in 5 years would mean a 0.02% increase in federal taxes. If we say 10 of these things strike the country in a year, and 50 over 5 years, then that would settle at a 1% increase in federal taxes to pay for natural disasters. This doesn't include forest fires, which are going to keep getting more and more out of control as long as we keep doing what we're doing; as in preventing natural fire cycles from occurring. I'm not going to go into detail regarding forest management in this edition. And now that we've nearly gotten to the end, I might as well come clean and tell you that the minimum income tax rate will likely have to be at least 30% – with 10% going to each level of government.

I don't know if you noticed, but I added something that I haven't yet mentioned into that last Article – low-income housing. The government can and should create money for low-income housing. They're already doing this but not at the rate they should be, and they're also charging too much for what they build. This is one industry that is guaranteed to eventually pay itself off while also helping the poor.

I left spending for things like the homeless out of that last article because an expenditure like that is likely never going to pay itself off. We can't create money for things that aren't unexpected (like natural disasters), or into programs that will never pay off that debt. The mentally ill and many of the homeless will likely always be employed or looked after in some form by the government. Therefore, expenditures like this need to be paid for by tax income.

I really want you to remember what I'm about to say – printing money is the most dangerous aspect of direct democracy. You must be hyper-vigilant with this power or the system fails. Okay, that's it about printing money.

After the first congressional election in which you get the majority, you have two years to make changes before the next election comes. If we can somehow get ⅔ control of Congress, then none of this matters, and the Constitution can be changed to give the people complete power over laws and taxes. As well as change the entire election process. But, getting ⅔ seems unlikely. So, we'll have to do things in these first two years to convince the other two teams that what we can accomplish with this system is for their benefit. The people that already voted for direct democracy are likely not going anywhere. They're the 2 cookie eaters that understand it takes short-term pain to produce long-term gain – they won't be scared off easily. But, we will still need to attract the others in order to create a bullet proof constitution.

I suggest after changing the laws surrounding the federal reserve, we immediately change laws surrounding resources. We give the resources to the people and spend whatever it takes to become resource independent. This would create an incredible amount of jobs and will definitely pay that investment off. I have a hard time believing that the majority from either team wouldn't want this.

You also need to enact a law, which should already exist, that prevents foreign entities from buying land or property, especially while the dollar is weak – keep your property affordable for your own citizens. Construction workers that will be affected by this law will become employed in the millions of infrastructure jobs that are going to start up.

We create laws that force factories (those that have no choice but to pollute) to sequester all emissions and we give them interest-free loans to build those structures. They then pay off those loans from the sale of waste carbon, which is then turned into synthetic fuel. We'll have to quickly build hydrogen and renewable energy plants in states where clean energy is abundant. The most efficient solution would be to build these structures close to the polluting factories and pump those emissions right into the hydrogen plants. We can transform abandoned factories and warehouses for lots of this. Be thrifty and don't spend like the current government does – as in building opulent structures on the most expensive real estate.

Eventually, we need to become carbon-neutral, instead of just recycling carbon that's been created from fossil fuels. But this is a good first step – we're building infrastructure that will eventually create a system where we only drill for oil or gas at a minimal level, and can produce all of the synthetic fuel we need while being carbon-neutral. Most importantly, there should be a carbon tax, that these companies pay, which covers the cost to offset those carbon emissions with the 'rocks-on-the-beach' method of storing CO_2 on the ocean floor – it should only cost about $12 a tonne...peanuts.

I've laid out the order in this book that I think we should work in. It starts with communication – if the owners of media conglomerates try to mess with free speech, then you take those companies away from the people that own them. You make a law to distinguish between news and opinion – a news show can't say news in its title if they can't prove that everything they're saying is a fact; otherwise, they get fined, big time. Maybe create another law, like Europe has, concerning privacy and data collection.

Then, you create laws that take profit out of energy production – it's a right of the people. We need to invest heavily into developing cold fusion – a 1% increase in federal tax, 40 billion dollars a year, would likely give us cold fusion in a decade. Many of our problems would then be solved. Remember, America spends almost 20 times that amount each year on the military. So, what I'm really saying is we need to get our priorities in order.

You create laws that mandate sustainable farming. Then, you move onto taxes. You make simple tax laws, like I describe in this book. You remove a lot of federal laws and give more power for legislation to districts and states. Then, you let the people decide on what they want to vote on next. You use the money from resources to immediately pay off the foreign debt that drunk Uncle Sam has racked up. You create new laws surrounding drugs and reform the entire prison system. You create the tax hunter, and you make a movie about an autistic hit-man that kills tax evaders...just checking to make sure you're still paying attention.

Who knows what's going to be the priority at that time? But shit is going to be hitting the fan if enough people have become brave enough to make this type of change. And I assure you, shit is going to hit the fan at some point. It's meant to happen to give you the courage to do this. Because no matter how hard and scary it will be in the beginning, with each passing day it will get easier.

The world will settle down – they'll realize that for the most part, it's business as usual in America. Then, you start making incremental changes. It's a scary thing, I'm not going to lie, and just writing this out makes me nervous. But it has to be done. You must get your country out of this downward spiral and become the beacon of hope that America is supposed to be – Drunk Uncle isn't going to do it for you.

If we act quickly, I believe it would only take 10 to 20 years to right the ship and become profitable. The longer we wait, the bigger that time frame becomes. If we wait 30 years, when the country is really collapsing, then I predict it will take at least 50 to 100 years before America becomes a functioning nation again. I'll be 70 by that point, and ready for death, so from a selfish standpoint, since I don't have any kids, I don't really need to worry. You parents and young adults are the ones that need to act on this, immediately. Let's move on to some of the problems we will encounter at the start.

When this party first gets power, the majority of people who voluntarily register are going to be those that voted for direct democracy. The other teams are likely going to be quite bitter and frightened – they're going to refuse to register. Therefore, it's quite possible that this initial group of registered voters will not make up the majority, and yet will be able to create all sorts of federal laws. You must refrain from making a bunch of federal laws before you get the majority of Americans registered and taking part. Once 90% of people are involved in the voting process, it will be very difficult to make federal laws, and that's how we evolve this system the fastest – by giving the smallest entities free reign to evolve, to innovate, and to make mistakes. The only federal laws you should make in the beginning are those that benefit the vast majority of people, like what I already talked about. Show the others the power that this system can wield in terms of bettering their lives and the long-term economy of America. You give them 18 months to register and then they get fined.

Some will still refuse to register. They will have such a distrust of government or fear of change that they'll be willing to die over this cause. If they're employed and paying taxes, or they have a driver's license, then they're going to get registered whether they like it or not. If they don't willingly do it, in order to update their information, then they should get fined. If they don't take part or give their vote to another party, then they'll continue to get fined. If they simply refuse to ever pay taxes, or contribute with their time and labor, then they'll end up going through the process that will eventually get them executed – three strikes and you're out.

I realize many people won't like me saying that, and by no means am I saying you have to take this path. But what else are you going to do with them? Are you going to let them not pay taxes? Continually put them in prison for not paying taxes? You want to spend money on these people instead of making money off of them? That's definitely one way to continue to go into debt, or force you to pay a lot more in taxes. Money for punishment can't be created, it has to come from tax income because there is nothing about punishment which involves investment into the future. I personally don't think it would take many executions before the others smartened up. If that thought bothers you, then you better be willing to pay more in taxes, or come up with a better solution. I really hope people out there have better solutions than what I've suggested. The last thing I want is to kill people, I just don't see another way of forcing laws on them – not when they'll be willing to die over their fear-based beliefs – and not pay a fortune in taxes, that should be going somewhere else.

To help with registration, you enlist high-school graduates. They volunteer and get paid $800 a month, with $20,000 guaranteed to go towards their education. If we could recruit a million teenagers, then they would just need to register 330 people each. There won't be any systems in place for them to grow food, do military service, or whatever else in these first couple of years, in order to get free education. Therefore, this will be the only immediate government service available to them, and they should only volunteer for it. We then need to work towards creating just one government account, which has everything on it, and that's the job that these teenagers would have. Let's also transfer over some of those clever NSA programmers and engineers to work on this. There should be absolutely no reason for a census to have to be done ever again. It will be a person's responsibility to update their info and it should be a simple one-step process.

Other major problems that we're going to encounter are deep red states that simply refuse to abandon their team. They want no part in direct democracy or new America. Plus, they're a little bit crazy and heavily armed. You can't force them to adopt this system, or they'll just dig in their heels further – they're itching for a civil war. They'll come around, eventually. They'll have to because they won't be able to create money. Not to mention, federal laws will be created without their input.

I can almost guarantee that the states that fight this transition of power the most will be the poorest and most uneducated states. We have to let them create laws that are important to them, like those involving abortion. If we want to get these red districts on board, then letting them create laws surrounding abortion is the best way to do that. We are going to need to compromise in order to make this work. Remember, those people will be forced to pay for left-wing policies that they don't want to pay for – they should be given something in return. I doubt there would be many states or a ton of districts that would make abortion illegal. This is not the issue to fall on our sword over, and it would do a lot of the heavy lifting in terms of getting these people involved in the system.

Let them create laws that will likely force the young to leave those districts, and we help those people to move. We also offer free abortions to women coming from districts or states that have made it illegal. Those districts will likely lose a lot of employment income because of these laws and they'll learn. Let them crash and burn and wait for them to accept help – they then lose their ability to make their own laws. We can't start a civil war over this new system. The only thing we can do is help the districts, that voted for direct democracy, that are stuck in these dying states. As well as support individuals who want to flee into neighboring states.

Then again, these districts or states would likely see an influx of pro-lifers moving there from districts that keep abortion legal. Let them live together and make laws that they all want – that's democracy. These places will live in the dark ages, they'll shun science and innovation, and they'll eventually collapse. The only laws we have to enforce on them are environmental protection laws. We have to let them go on this regressive path because they won't accept anything else until they learn these lessons for themselves.

Another issue is going to be getting people on board who will likely lose their jobs because of the changes we'd be making. They'll need to be convinced that this is going to be in their best interests, in the long term. They have to know that we'll train them in something else and there will be plenty of jobs available – they aren't going to be left out in the pasture to die. Many individuals will sacrifice a healthy planet and sustainable society because of fear over their own immediate survival. How do we replace that fear with logic? It won't be easy and it's all going to come down to actually showing them – no amount of reasoning will snap them out of their fear-based thinking patterns. We show them by quickly creating a ton of infrastructure jobs that will heal America and the environment – who wouldn't want that?

This process isn't going to be all sunshine and lollipops – nothing good ever comes that easily. Just be patient and know that they're blinded by fear. They've been fed misinformation by media outlets. They won't realize that they'll actually be able to create more laws that benefit them with this system than with their current team. We have to show them that this is possible and allow them to make their own laws...within reason.

We should be able to create an efficient system where we pay the same amount of taxes but get a lot more done...maybe just a slight increase in taxes...in the beginning. We'll show them that this system is the best way to ensure their survival and ability to feed their families. They'll come around, eventually.

The Constitution is a great thing; it helped America become the first democratic nation. Well, technically that was Greece. And they had their own hero who rose up with the power of the people to change the Constitution – as you will as well. There's no question that the Constitution needs to evolve and be rewritten. This current form of governance is quite obviously corrupted, not to mention extremely wasteful and inefficient. If we do this right, then we'll eventually have the numbers to write that new Constitution. I'm going to spread ideas, but I'm not your champion. If you spread this book, and these ideas to enough people, then I can guarantee that that person will rise up. They will read this book and they'll become an unstoppable force. He or she may already be in the spotlight. Maybe it's you!

They are brave and not afraid of death, especially when it comes to saving their country and the world. They might already be a billionaire who isn't afraid of paying their fair share – that would be ideal. They will become a hero for the planet. I'm pretty sure there's a billionaire out there who's more concerned with being a hero and saving the world than he or she is with making more money. Their names will be written in the history books for millennia as the person that started the movement towards world peace. I can see it, can't you?

If America isn't ready for this, if America shuns these ideas and this call to action, then I suppose I'll have to wait until more young people come of age – or until more people realize the disaster that their government has become. Maybe another country will jump all over this and show America how it's done. Maybe it'll be Canada. I sure hope you don't let anyone do that, America! YOU'RE NUMBER ONE! Remember? Be number one.

On that note, I'd like to send a personal message to my birth country. If Canada was to adopt direct democracy and take control of its resources, then it could become a very wealthy nation, instead of being mired in some of the highest per capita debt on the planet. But there would be a couple hurdles to overcome: the first is the fact that we are part of the Commonwealth, which means we have to get Royal assent for any legislation. That's an easy fix if they refuse what we want, by simply leaving the Commonwealth. The second issue is Canada's insane system of appointing senators for life (until they reach the age of 75), which most Canadians aren't even aware of.

The Prime Minister appoints these lifetime senators and they are not elected, yet they serve the same role in passing laws as America's senators. If the Canadian Senate denied any law surrounding direct democracy, then Canadians must revolt – I will be at the front of the line. There is no form of democracy, that any sane individual could imagine, in which the people can't elect those responsible for passing new laws. Let's wait and see what the Senate does when our only elected officials pass this bill onto them. If they reject direct democracy, then we'll just have to pretend like our hockey team lost, and that will get people out on the streets to riot. Although, in this case I would say that we can ignore our constitution and simply disband the Senate. What power would they actually have to prevent this from happening? The military or the police? I don't think so. This isn't even primitive democracy in Canada, and therefore the rules of our constitution don't need to be followed.

On that note, after picking a fight with my own government, I guess it's time to wrap this up. It's been a blast spending time with you wonderful folks. I really enjoyed writing this book, and I'll enjoy chatting with all of you on Twitter, you'll see my info at the end – I'm going to talk to everyone that brings up valid points. If you don't have Twitter, then get it – how else are we going to talk? I honestly believe Twitter is a great tool for communication and for uniting the masses. The fact that they are taking on the President and fighting for truth is very telling of their CEO, whom I think is a good human. Just don't get caught up in the bullshit – use it for good, not to spread hate and strife.

I gave up social media when I started writing, because it was an unnecessary distraction. But I'm diving back into the mayhem for this purpose. If you're one of the first people to read this and you see that my social media accounts are lacking, that's why. Let's build them up with interesting ideas. Social media is basically going to be my full-time job for the next little while, and my part time job indefinitely.

I desperately want to hear what you think won't work and whether you have other solutions. What I don't want to hear is a fear of change that keeps you going on this current path. I also don't want to hear you objecting to my suggestions without a different plan – problems and solutions only, not simply objections. This is just the starting point. The discussions and thought that will go into fixing the world all come after this. There will be more editions of this book, and the new ideas will all stem from what we come up with together.

Many more minds will be able to accomplish so much more than just mine alone. I can't foresee all of the problems that will come from my suggestions. But with all of us putting our heads together, I bet we'll be able to foresee a lot of them and prevent many problems before they start.

There are nine Articles for our new Constitution in this book. I'm pretty sure it's supposed to be 10...that's just a hunch. I imagine the last Article will have something to do with spreading wealth and resources among the districts and states. I'm going to leave that one up to the people to figure out. The final edition of this book will essentially be like a bible for direct democracy and a sustainable world, that we all write together, and we're going to perfect the 10 Articles for our bible. We are going to create a much simpler Constitution and form of governance that is able to adapt and make changes more efficiently. Most importantly, we won't make that final edition as goofy as this one.

If any teachers around the world want to use this book for political science, environmental, or economics courses etc., then be my guest. Photocopy certain pages or do whatever it takes – you don't have to make everyone buy the book. You could spend many lectures going through these problems and how to fix them, if we had direct democracy. As well as figuring out the money it might actually cost. This book was purposefully written to be an easy and engaging read for young people, so let's figure out a way to get young people to read it. My stats and numbers are likely not 100% accurate, as I only used Google to research. The numbers aren't what's important here, addressing the problems and figuring out how to fix them are all that matters. I'm also likely completely wrong and off-base on some things, so help me fix that.

I give anyone permission to pirate this book, if it means spreading these ideas – I won't go after anyone for copyright infringement...unless you're selling it. I need money, obviously, but getting people to think about a better future is more important than the money. If you can spare a few dollars, then buy the e-book.

You'd think that governments should be doing a better job at fixing the problems of the world, and they should be, but they're not – so we will. Just do your job, you lazy shit. Just kidding, I love you. You got this far and you're already a hero of the political revolution that's coming...as long as you do your job and spread these ideas. Eat your second cookie after you do it, as a reward. You earned it.

Exciting times are ahead – don't focus on the doom and gloom. It's just the cycle of life, and right now we're on a downward turn. We can halt it as quickly or as slowly as you care to act. I'm going to be doing everything I can to get things moving quickly, but I need your help. Nothing happens without each and every individual reading this book and spreading it to as many people as you can. Just do one job, but do it well, and you'll play a huge role in saving this planet.

Just don't tell any Americans, that you get to read this book, that I'm Canadian. Nobody wants to hear what's wrong with their country from a foreigner. I would personally love to hear solutions from Americans on how to fix problems in Canada, but you don't give a shit what we're doing. So, let's keep the focus on you. But, let's change this terrifying reality show going on in American politics from, HERE COMES HONEY BOO BOO: Apocalypse Edition, to, EXTREME MAKEOVER: Political Edition.

Although, it would be must-see TV to watch Honey Boo Boo eat a human. Damn, now I really want to watch that. On second thought, whatever you want to do, I'm cool with.

A Personal Message to You

Battling depression is going to become a large part of the future, as it already is now. As the world becomes more populated and competitive, it's going to become harder and harder to accomplish those difficult dreams that you set out for yourself as a kid. But taking drugs, whether legal or illegal, will never be the solution to this problem; yet, I fear that having a drugged-out majority population is a battle that we're going to have to face in the not too distant future.

There's an ideal in America that anyone can become wealthy just from hard work. I hate to break it to you, but that's simply not true. Maybe it used to be, but it's never been that way in my lifetime. I'm sure many of you out there already work hard, and you can barely get ahead. Hard work is not the only thing it takes – to get ahead takes a great deal of sacrifice.

In fact, not only sacrifice but also something special about you. Maybe you're stunningly beautiful, highly intelligent, motivated beyond imagination, incredibly disciplined, maybe you have a creative gift, have an ambition that can't be stifled, or you have zero fear and go after everything you want with a fiery drive. There needs to be something else besides hard work. Everyone has a talent in them, but most haven't figured out what that is. Figure out what your talent is and focus on that. You already know what it is...deep inside. If you really don't know, then get your time of birth and study Astrology – it'll help you figure it out.

Where did this idea that everyone needs to be rich to be happy even come from? Have you noticed celebrities? Do they all seem happy to you with their drug addictions and battles with depression that they face themselves? Stop worrying about what others have that you want. I realize that's a far easier thing to say than do, especially in this age of social media. Everyone struggles with this. Everyone has an incredible battle to face; even though it seems that some have an easy life, they still face battles that are just as hard to them as your actual difficult battles are for you. Worry about your own growth and your own goals.

If your dream is to buy a house, but you have no idea how to get there (you're just treading water as it is), then you're going to have to sacrifice. You're going to have to get another job and do absolutely nothing else for however long it takes you to save up for a down payment. Better yet, take a loan out to get trained in a better paying job. Don't be afraid to learn new skills, remember?

If you want to become a musician, an actor, a writer, or a painter, etc., then you're going to have to sacrifice. You're going to have to stop spending your money on socializing every weekend so that you can work less and practice. You've got to work hard, every single day, towards your craft, with a laser focus in accomplishing your goals, one step at a time. You have to believe that there's absolutely nothing else you could possibly do with your life, and no amount of rejection will ever stop you. Those are the only people that ever become successful in those types of competitive pursuits. You also need to be adaptable. If something isn't working, then you need to develop new strategies. If you continue to do these things, and you never give up, then you'll reach some form of success, no matter how long it takes – that's a guarantee that life gives you.

If that doesn't sound like something you're willing to do, then don't worry about it. There's absolutely nothing wrong with living an average life. You've got challenges and growth that need to be addressed, no matter what stage of life you're at. Focus on those things and find an outlet that makes you happy. Express yourself, as Madonna says. Challenge yourself and don't shrink away from the hard work or the situations that make you nervous – when you know that getting through it will benefit you in the long run. Always ask yourself, 'what's the worst that could happen?' I will guarantee it'll never be worse than the regret of not trying.

If you feel like you're in a rut, then stop being ruled by the fear of what could go wrong if you chase your dreams. If a thought never leaves you alone about what you should be doing, then that's something that you should be doing, no question. Unless that thought involves hurting others, don't do that...go get a virgin sex robot to distract you.

Let go of your fears and don't get tied down by comforts – comfort kills dreams. Take a leap of faith, and the universe will guide you to where you need to be – even if it's not where you thought you should be. Trust in your abilities, because we all come here equipped with exactly what we need to overcome the obstacles put in front of us.

Just please don't take drugs to deal with your depression. That will only sink you further and further into a pit that you'll later have to dig yourself out of. If you need to release traumatic events or emotional injuries, then I highly suggest you write a book, like I did, and let it all out.

And then let someone read it, even a stranger. You wouldn't believe the cathartic release of just doing something like that can create. If you're bored, then you're going to have to make yourself uncomfortable to get out of that rut.

You already know what you should be doing. Don't let fear dictate your life. Let go of the past. Let go of the hatred and the anger that people different from you create – everyone suffers from this in varying degrees. Fear, hatred and anger bring your frequency down, and don't allow you to connect to your higher self. And don't beat yourself up too much when you screw up...even multiple times with the same mistake. Just pick yourself up and continually try to do better. That's all anyone can ask out of any life they lead – just always try and do better the next time. If you do that, you'll be exactly where you need to be. And that's the only purpose of life you need to worry about. Above all, the greatest defense against depression is hope and love. I love you for reading this. Now go do your job and let's create a world full of hope for a better future.

About the Author

I could talk about my accolades but all of it is meaningless. The only thing that matters is what I plan to do once I have a platform to be heard. I wrote this book to give society solutions needed to fix the mess we're all in, but I don't want to be known as a writer. Books and movies are simply tools that I will use to spread ideas and to fund a revolution. I hope to eventually be known as a philanthropist, businessman and innovator. Above all, I hope to be known as a revolutionary. Everything I do in life will be with the goal of world peace in mind. My past or my future mean nothing without that mission. I am here to share ideas and to create a platform to unite. Only a united population can change the world. I am nothing without you.

Follow me on Twitter and Instagram: @tylertrue1980